Little Outlaws, Dirty Angels

Finding freedom in the new South Africa

Tom Hewitt

Hodder & Stoughton
LONDON SYDNEY AUCKLAND

British Library Cataloguing in Publication Data
A record for this book is available from the British Library

ISBN 0 340 73518 X

Typeset by Hewer Text Ltd, Edinburgh
Printed and bound in Great Britain by Clays Ltd, St Ives plc

Hodder and Stoughton Ltd
A Division of Hodder Headline PLC
338 Euston Road
London NW1 3BH

Dear Jane,

Thankyou for a wonderful evening. Its great to meet someone so dedicated to South Africa

**Little Outlaws,
Dirty Angels**

Siyabonga,

[signature]

'An extraordinary story from an extra ordinary bloke.'

Simon Mayo

'I'm sure Tom would not want to be put on any kind of pedestal, but there's no doubt that his story is inspirational. His work with the street kids is a tangible expression of the Kingdom of God – let those who read this book be provoked "to do" as well.'

Jenny Baker
CARE for Education

Tom is dynamic at what he does and comes at a time when streetwork in Durban needs strong servant leadership and from what I see this is something he does best. Kids love him and team members respect him – his heart and passion seem to motivate those around him. As we seek to serve Tom, I pray that we will write letters of hope and promise on each other's lives and together find the courage to love faithfully and be a concrete presence to the poor.'

Robyn Hemmens
Youth for Christ, Durban

'Tom Hewitt is an example to his generation. This story will inspire and motivate those who want to act upon their dreams of a world where justice and mercy become the wave that we surf.'

Rt. Rev. James Jones
Bishop of Liverpool

'As the new South Africa inherited its present, Tom Hewitt has been working with its future. The story of the street kids in South Africa can't fail to make compelling reading. And Tom can tell his story as well as anyone.

Tom Hewitt's story is a tribute to Tom. More importantly, it is a challenge to the rest of us. When Jesus talked about children and said "the Kingdom of God belongs to such as these" he wasn't joking! How each generation treats its children and young people is one of the most important tests by which all of us will be judged.'

Simon Hughes MP
(North Southwark & Bermondsey)

'I've met Tom Hewitt and believe me he's impressive. A clear focus and genuine well-balanced dedication are usually assets of mature years, but Tom is young and his story gives my optimism a huge boost. His work among the street kids of South Africa is extraordinary and if you're cynical about the level of commitment and initiative of today's generation this book will restore your perspective.'

Sir Cliff Richard

Contents

Author's acknowledgments

To my father and mother Garth and Gill – thank you for all your love and support. I love you both more than you could imagine!

Thanks to Ben and Joe for just being my brothers and best friends and to Abi for being such a loyal and loving sister. I love you loads. To my grandmothers Amy Summer and Daffodil Hewitt, thank you for your hours of prayer and support.

Thanks to my editor Viv Wickham and to the Amos Trust trustees, for believing in me, supporting and encouraging me, and for their commitment to street children and social justice. Special thanks to Sue Plater, my line manager, for being a real support and encouragement.

Thanks to Simon and Hilary Mayo, Tony Neeves (for spiritual guidance!), and the Neeves family for being around as far back as my memory goes. To all the Amos supporters and those who have supported me – thank you for making my work possible. Beki Bateson – thanks for always being there behind the scenes, propping me up. You are indeed a great friend as well as a dynamic team mate. Thanks also to Claire Dowding in the office.

Thanks to David Bracewell and the congregation of St. Saviour's, Guildford; my best mate Kristen Meadows, Peter, and the Meadows family; Steve "peanut" Bewes; Jeremy "Les" Radcliffe; Mark "plain lazy" Hagley; Phil "surfing guru and tour guide" Sheffield; Diane Mills; Sir Cliff Richard; Andrew and Linda Southwood; Peter Rattu and all the students at Sharnbrook school, and the "Duke and Duchess of Durrington"!

In South Africa:

Patrick, Hayley and Kayla Lottering – thanks for your wonderful friendship and for helping me so much through your hospitality and love. Mike Nomtoto, "Bra Mike", you are a friend forever. Nosimo Kantyo – thanks for your support and love for the kids. Auntie Maggie – I love you lots, Auntie! Children of Isaiah 58, I love you forever and think and pray for you always. Children of Deerfield and Gatesway, keep up the faith, I love you.

To my friends Stanley and Lindile, remain agents of peace and justice. Thanks to Caesar Molebatsi for encouragement and support; to Comrade Blom and the African National Congress; Promise; Nkosinathi; Bandile and all at Divine Life Center in Zwelitsha for loving the children and great gospel music! Thanks to Brian and Pauline Cape, Andy and Rose at Miracle House Shelter in Aliwal North, and Brad Cuff (Q-bay rules)! Thanks to Streetwise Shelter, Durban, especially Sister Helena, Sisi Ntuthu, and Bheki. Also to Siyakhiwa Shelter, Durban, especially Mrs. Ndaba, Sisi Nonhlanhla and Eugene, and to YFC Durban, especially Sisi Lindiwe and Mandy. Special thanks to Robyn Hemmens for tirelessly reading the manuscript and for being a friend and colleague with a passion for serving street children. Thanks to all at the Coffee Shop on Dairy Beach, Durban where most of this story was written.

This book is written in memory of Siseko Sisulu, who's death shook me, and for Comrade Cecil Dita, a profound thinker, a selfless fighter of the people's struggle and a wise, supportive friend. Also for my grandfathers Thomas Hewitt and Gerald Sumner, who was the kindest man I have ever met and a true hero of mine.

Foreword by Simon Mayo

So here's the deal. As I write, Michael Caine is looking very happy with his Golden Globes, Tom Hanks is getting excited about receiving his umpteenth Oscar nomination and Robbie Williams is contemplating a record number of Brit Awards. And well done indeed to all of them because, to state the bloomin' obvious, they are all fantastically talented and I might have to interview one or all of them soon.

These are probably some of the most famous people on the planet – certainly some of the most lauded and applauded. These are CELEBRITIES. A strange concept at the best of times, though one which has always been with us. Since human beings learned to worship, adore and be jealous, we have put people on pedestals. What they do when they get there is up to them but it is us who put them there in the first place . . . If you are wondering what this has to do with Tom Hewitt and this book be patient, I'm coming to that.

So imagine, if you will, another awards ceremony. This one is to be held at Madison Square Gardens and will be hosted by Billy Crystal and Eddie Izzard (it's my foreword and I'll choose who I want). It costs £500 a ticket and everybody wants to be there – presidents, prime ministers, princes and princesses, anyone whose title begins with a P, movie stars, rock stars and sports stars. *Hello* magazine has paid squillions for the rights to take all the pictures. REM are doing the cabaret, Steven Spielberg is directing the video and Raymond Blanc is cooking.

But here's a strange thing. According to the programme

(introduction by Louis de Bernieres), the categories are unusual. Unexpected. Decidedly odd.

'Most committed nurse'

'Best performance under pressure by a youth worker'

'Most extraordinary peace negotiator'

'Most sacrificial career move'

'Most disarming joke performed with a knife at your throat'

As each recipient makes their way to the podium, the audience stands, the cameras flash and the applause is deafening. The speeches are witty, self-effacing and political dynamite. The world leaders in attendance realise the destructive manner of their policies, which have made everything worse, and change their ways. The millionaire superstars give away their fortunes, Tom Hanks *really does* cry this time, the lion lies down with the lamb, and everyone leaves to the sound of new ploughshares being made.

Sorry, I'm getting a bit carried away. But you get the picture. Those of us who could no more be Tom Hewitt than be a high-wire trapeze artist can only read this book and marvel. This is life on a front line way beyond most of our experiences. The journey from Guildford, Surrey to the streets of Durban is not the obvious one for a bloke with Tom's talents (I blame the parents) but one for which countless South Africans will be eternally grateful.

I'm not sure how many awards Tom picks up at my fantasy ceremony, but it would be armfuls. And I'm on my seat yelling!

Simon Mayo

EASTERN COAST OF SOUTH AFRICA

ORANGE FREE STATE

KWA-ZULU NATAL

LESOTHO

PIETERMARITZBURG

● **DURBAN**

ALIWAL NORTH

EASTERN CAPE

UMTATA

INDIAN OCEAN

KING WILLIAM'S TOWN ● BISHO

● **EAST LONDON**

● PORT ELIZABETH

They are orphaned by our opulence, they are homeless by our greed;
The rich world makes its living through the poor world on its knees.
A nation roams the streets tonight, you'll see them everywhere,
One hundred million children, an army of despair.

Little outlaws are on the streets, dirty angels in full flight.
They are running out of fear, they are fighting to survive.
Little outlaws, who'll protect you? Where will you sleep tonight?
Little outlaws on the streets, dirty angels in full flight.

From the song *Little Outlaws, Dirty Angels*
by Garth Hewitt

1 They killed him on the streets

'Tom, it's Siseko, there is so much blood, please come now, please.' It was Boy-Boy. His voice was trembling, he was in shock. He paused.

'Where are you?' I asked. I knew full well that when a street child called from a public phone it would be a matter of seconds before the money ran out, so it was vital to establish their whereabouts.

'We are at the bridge. You know, the one we sleep under.'

With that I hung up. We had an emergency. I quickly put on a pair of shorts, fumbled for my shoes, T-shirt and car keys and headed for my pick-up truck. As I drove I was praying, 'Please Lord, I don't know what's going on but I pray for your help. Be with Siseko and the boys.'

The streets were empty; I drove like a madman. As I pulled up to the boys I noticed the ambulance pulling away.

'Good,' I thought. 'The boys have done the right thing by contacting the emergency services.' The boys ran up to me and gave me a garbled description of what had happened. Siseko had been found nearby with his trousers undone and his head smashed in by a large rock. I stumbled down to the disused railway line. Sure enough there was a large rock with skin and blood on it. There was blood everywhere on the ground and next to it Siseko's little wallet that he had found on the streets. He used to keep it to put the few cents in that kind passers-by would give him.

The boys climbed into the front and back of the pick-up truck and we raced up to the hospital. A million thoughts went through my head as we sat in silence on the short drive to the hospital. Is he going to die? Could it be true? Why hadn't he been with the other children? Who had done this? Had he been raped? Was it really serious or just a lot of blood? Question after question. The ride seemed endless.

We were all too familiar with the casualty ward at the Frere Hospital in East London, South Africa. Countless times I'd waited while the kids were sewn up after being stabbed, or X-rayed after having been hit by cars or beaten up. Many times I had sat outside in the waiting-room after bringing in young girls who had been raped, listening to their sobs and cries as they endured the awful degrading examination, each sob penetrating deep into my heart. What condition would Siseko be in when we arrived at the hospital?

Siseko Sisulu came from a large family that lived in the Ziphunzana area of Duncan Village township in East London, South Africa. He didn't know his father and his mother was unemployed. She had no home of her own so she stayed in a tin shack situated behind a small two-room house belonging to her relatives. She had had a hard life of poverty and from an early age Siseko had learned how to fend for himself in the squatter camp. However, things were tough. A meal was hard to come by and violence was rife in the area. Children were often affected by the situation and became prime targets for abuse. Some kids just endured the townships; others looked for a way out, a better life.

At the age of thirteen, Siseko started to look outside the township for a life of fun and to escape from the 'ghetto life'. Why not? The city streets looked so clean, had so many shops, so many rich clean people. It was exciting and, what's more, there were other children there. It wasn't long before he was enjoying the camaraderie of a group of children living on the streets. Mostly they were slightly older than Siseko and had been there for a while; they seemed so streetwise. They knew how to survive and how to dodge the dreaded city police and have fun at the same time. The leader of the group was a 16-year-old called Boy-Boy, a tough character yet with a very defined streak of compassion for the younger children. He had been a street child for most of his life. He had spent time in prison on a number of occasions, most recently for rape but had escaped by making a mad dash out from the court building at his trial, long since forgotten by the authorities.

Boy-Boy welcomed Siseko into their group. A gang or group meant protection on the dangerous streets. There were about ten main children in the group but that number fluctuated. Boy-Boy's best friend was a boy nicknamed Pinnochio who was also wanted for rape. Simthembele, another friend, was softer but tough enough to handle the streets. Munstu was slightly older and lived his entire life sniffing benzine from a rag. He was always high, never violent, and often funny. Munstu was a psychological wreck at the age of nineteen. The constant sniffing of benzine (thinners) as a means to escape the realities of his life had left him almost unable to use his legs properly. However, he also had a very caring heart and had been responsible for taking children off the streets, saying that they were too young to be there.

Then there were the girls: Felicia, Nomsa, Nora and Thandi. They ranged between the ages of eleven and sixteen and their main role was to support the group through prostitution and to be girlfriends to the older boys. Night after night they would stand on a certain street corner waiting to be picked up, waiting for that little bit of money that came from selling their dignity and self-respect. They looked at little Siseko affectionately. Often street girls are very kind and compassionate toward the little street boys because, first, many of them grew up with younger brothers and sisters and, second, because these boys are not after them sexually. They are easy-going and would never hurt these girls. They are good fun. Siseko was harmless and at the same time a good companion – he fitted in just fine.

Siseko was protected; everyone loved him and besides he

had a cute face. Maybe the white people would give him some money. They liked to give a few cents to a small child. It made them feel good. Once that child reached puberty, though, he was viewed as a threat and the whites would seldom feel compassion for him. Siseko would also be used to generate money in another devastating way. There were men in town who would pay money to have sexual favours done to them by small boys. He could earn up to 5 or 10 rand for doing this. Siseko was an asset to the group.

Once on the streets Siseko began to look like your stereotypical street kid. No matter what colour a person's clothes are, when they are never washed they always look a dirty greyish colour. When I first met Siseko he used to wear a filthy old trench coat, much too big for him, with an array of T-shirts and jumpers to keep him warm. He would wear all his clothes at once! It was the only way he could keep them all. He wore an old pair of trousers held together with a piece of string and had no shoes. His feet were as tough as leather, cracked with layers of dirt and dry with damaged and broken nails. If you stood close enough to him you could smell the stench of body odour. His hair was short but unkempt and he often wore a 'tea cosy' hat on his head. He had a large smile exposing his white teeth. His eyes were wide open; the streets were new and exciting for him. However, they grew lazy as he started to depend upon the sniffing of benzine. The more time children spend on the streets the more they begin to realise that it is not fun, and that survival often depends on surrendering their dignity. It is not surprising that sniffing glue or benzine becomes their escape and indeed their life.

Siseko's arrival on the streets happened during my time at Isaiah 58. Isaiah 58 Children's Village is a home that caters for street children – abandoned and abused children as well as those growing up on the rubbish dumps. Whenever a new child came on to the streets it became a priority of mine to develop a relationship with that child and to try and get that child off the streets. The sooner the better, before they really got into the street scene. I knew all of the children in the group that Siseko joined and these children introduced me to Siseko when he arrived among them. Siseko was fairly typical of newcomers to the streets. He was vibrant and extremely friendly and used to run after my car, flagging it down whenever he saw it passing. I used to stop and talk with Siseko and spent time getting to know him. I chatted to Siseko about his past and we talked about life on the streets. He wanted to leave but he wasn't sure about this big place called 'Isaiah'. He was used to fending for himself. The thought of living with rules and regulations and 120 other kids was certainly daunting for him.

Eventually I persuaded him to come along and meet the chief housemother who was affectionately known to everyone as Auntie Maggie. Auntie Maggie is a black woman from the surrounding area, probably now in her early sixties. She is a strong, larger-than-life character which fits her physical make-up, and she has devoted her life to serving the children of Isaiah 58. She is employed as housemother to them and is a committed Christian. Auntie Maggie is the backbone of Isaiah 58 and has the responsibility of keeping law and order as well as being a mother to all the children. She was often nervous when I used to bring the roughest street children to Isaiah. After all, it was easy for me because I could go home to peace and quiet at the end of the day. She was there twenty-four hours a day, seven days a week – it was her life. Auntie Maggie welcomed an even more wary Siseko to the project. He had a look round, and soon got over the embarrassment of 120 sets of children's eyes staring softly at him; after all they had all been there once. Contact had been made – Siseko was now familiar with Isaiah. He wouldn't stay yet, however. With some children who hadn't yet felt the dangers of the streets, it took time and several visits before they stayed.

Siseko came back to Isaiah a couple of times and really

enjoyed himself; this was part of the process. He was nearly ready to stay, nearly ready for that big jump in the life of a street child. However, sadly, the streets were going to dictate his future. I often think if only I had been firmer, if only I had got him off the streets sooner, if only I had spent even more time with him, prayed harder, if only, if only . . .

'I'm sorry. We tried our best,' the doctor said gently. He was overworked and had had a tough night. The bags under his eyes told the story, set against his white face. His words were, however, strangely comforting even though we were being told that there was nothing he could do. He was admitting defeat, yet I really felt that the words came from his heart with compassion. Somebody had actually tried to help Siseko. That comforted me, it showed that he had meant something. Siseko had been raped and beaten almost to death. He had swelling to his brain and was only kept alive by machine – he wasn't going to wake up again.

Boy-Boy was silently crying in despair – he really loved Siseko. Joseph – a hardened street boy who was also addicted to sniffing glue – retreated into himself, into a reclusive world that he often escaped to. I did not cry – now was not the time. I held the children. There are no words to describe the feeling of desolation that those kids were going through. Nobody was tough at that moment, nobody was afraid to cry or to show their emotions – the boys were exposed and beginning to realise their own vulnerability. They were scared, but more than that they were mourning the imminent loss of a close friend, a younger brother.

It was now 8 o'clock in the morning. I went home to change. It was then it hit me, as I was changing my clothes. I collapsed into a heap on the floor and cried out, asking God, 'Why?' I cried a lot, I mourned. I missed Siseko already, it hurt so much. I had never cried like that before, but it seemed to enable me to get to the next stage of handling the situation. It was like breaking through a barrier. I needed to be strong in support for the kids, all of whom needed to be shown God's love at that time. But to be able to do this I needed to pour out my feelings to God and to believe that it would be out of my own weakness and brokenness that I would find strength. I knew that God would equip me for the next stage.

I went back to the hospital with the children who wanted to see Siseko one last time although, with the swelling to his brain, Siseko didn't look much like his former self. We started to pray openly in the ICU ward. We prayed to God for him and spoke into his ears about the realities of Jesus. The boys went but I stayed to pray with him on my own. I sat and stroked his warm head. I chatted to him and spoke of all that God had in store for him. I spoke of heaven and Jesus. He never knew much about Jesus, except that he knew that I was a Christian and he showed some interest in Jesus. He was so young. As I prayed I felt that it was a golden moment, a spiritual moment. I felt that although unconscious, Siseko's spirit was very much alive. I wanted him to know that I loved him and, more importantly, that God valued and loved him and was waiting on the other side with his arms wide open to give him compassion and warmth.

They kept Siseko alive for as long as possible. It seemed that there was no one else to hold his hand in his last moments. He deserved at least this; he deserved someone to be affected by his death. He was a child who mattered. I decided I would take on the emotional responsibility of a parent to him. In his last moments someone was there, someone prayed and cried. His death caused a ripple in society; it wasn't ignored. Soon after midnight I felt it was time to say goodbye. I held his warm hand, kissed him and said, 'My boy, Jesus loves you and so do I.' I went straight home and had been asleep for just a few minutes when the phone rang. It was the nurse.

'I'm sorry,' she said. 'He just gave up at about one o'clock.'

'Thank you for all you've done,' I said. Then, just as I lay there, a strange peace came over me. I prayed a few words and fell into a deep sleep.

Siseko was a victim of the streets, deeply loved by God yet ignored by society. His life and death had a great effect on my life both vocationally and personally. I really felt the pain of his death and it made me determined to give my best to the street children of South Africa. This 14-year-old boy reminded me that God had a job for me to do, yet only through relying on him would I have the strength to do it. I was going to see many moving and disturbing images, and would have to deal with many harrowing situations and come up against some of the toughest opposition possible. Satan revels in the fact that kids live in such appalling conditions and suffer these terrible abuses. Going against this flow with God's help was certainly going to touch a nerve.

2 Catch a wave and you're sitting on top of the world!

'Yes, there's surf!' I would shout excitedly as our car came round the corner, bringing Polzeath beach into sight. My whole day depended on whether there were waves. If there was the slightest wave I would spend my entire day, regardless of the cold, trying to learn the basics of surfing.

My parents were encouraging, but they were probably wondering how on earth their son got into surfing, of all things. I can hear my mum now, saying, 'Do be careful out there!' For my father it was the beginning of sitting on endless beaches on different sides of the globe watching me surf and worrying about drowning, sharks and the thought of having to swim out and rescue me.

I was fifteen at the time and I could not believe that there was any other sport as beautiful as surfing. I became fascinated with watching waves break and during school lessons I would spend my entire time reliving waves that I had surfed, or dreaming of doing difficult manoeuvres on big waves.

I began to read surfing magazines religiously, collecting every single one monthly. These magazines covered most surfing spots around the world and really opened up my mind to the wealth of beautiful places, magnificent beaches and unbelievable surfing breaks. I think it was from those magazines that I became so interested in travelling, and so depressed about living in Guildford!

I dreamt about travelling the world. We did out best in England to make surfing possible but it just didn't seem like real surfing. After all, we had to wear ridiculously thick wet suits and the waves were very small. It was not exactly the surfing life of palm trees, warm water and endless tubes! I used to see the surfers in the magazines and the videos. They would be sun-tanned, well-built, surfing the best waves in the world in warm water. I dreamt of surfing in warm climates, of living in a place which had real surf and where surfing was a part of life.

Growing up in Guildford, I was the only surfer that I knew. It's hardly surprising, as it was over an hour to the nearest surfing spot – in my case, East Wittering, which unfortunately had waves only during winter. However, by the age of sixteen I would go down to East Wittering every weekend in the hope of finding surf. Admittedly, it wasn't real surf, usually a frothy chop whipped up by strong south-westerly gales. I met up with another surfing fanatic called Phil Sheffield who was about seven years older than me and had a camper van. We soon became very good friends and embarked together on a quest for finding surf.

During winter Phil and I would drive around the south coast from Brighton to Bournemouth and sometimes as far as Kimmeridge Bay looking for ridable surf. It was good fun, always off in the van, dreaming together of surfing far-off places. We used to sleep in the camper van and I remember on the coldest winter days putting on our wet suits, boots, gloves and balaclavas and paddling out into the freezing English Channel, all the while screaming, shouting and laughing to each other. We would sit out in the 'line-up' (the place just beyond where the waves start breaking) cracking jokes and waiting for a decent wave to come through, knowing that we had about an hour before hypothermia would set in! We were not good surfers at the time but I had some of the best times of my life, chasing a dream. Twelve years later we are still very close friends, and both still surf!

It was the family holidays in Cornwall that really helped me learn to surf. We used to go to the little surfing town of

Polzeath where I would spend every day surfing. Sometimes we would go to Newquay, which was a real treat for me because it was a surfing Mecca with lots of surf shops where I could spend hours wandering around. My dad, however, a lover of Cornwall, hated it because it was so busy and constantly referred to summer in Newquay as hell!

Surfing was indeed my love and I knew that one day I was going to surf real waves somewhere warm but until then I battled on in Cornwall and along the south coast. After about two years there was quite a group of us who surfed together, including my brother Ben. One time, when I was in the sixth form, I decided to race down to Wittering because there was surf that day. I loaded up our surfboards and wet suits and arranged to meet Ben who waited in his school uniform outside his school. We bunked off school and spent the whole day surfing. It was great, that is until we got back home. My mother had asked one of Ben's friends – a boy called Tim – where Ben was after school and, without thinking, Tim replied, 'Oh yeah, didn't the boys go surfing today?' We were dead!

I was born in Maidstone, Kent – a town that I know little about, perhaps because before my first birthday my parents had moved to Ealing in West London, where I grew up. I was given the names Thomas Luther Hewitt at birth. The name Thomas came from my grandfather, a tough Newcastle coalminer who had been part of a gang that happened upon a Christian meeting in Newcastle. They went along to break it up; however, the Lord had a different plan. Instead of causing havoc, Thomas and his fellow gang members ended up giving their lives to the Lord. Thomas went on to become an Anglican priest, teaching himself to read and write in the process. He was a determined young man who then earned himself a degree in theology and for the rest of his life deeply valued the gift of education. Each of my names is something symbolic to me and often helps me on the ever-continuing and unfolding journey of finding out

who I really am and what my purpose is in the global
community.

When my father was seventeen years old he heard that the
black civil rights leader Dr Martin Luther King would be in
London to speak at St Paul's Cathedral. He was thrilled at
the thought of hearing this great man speak but couldn't
find anyone to go along with him. None of his friends
wanted to go, so he went on his own. This event was not
only to change my father's life, particularly in the long run,
but to greatly influence me and indirectly contribute to my
identity.

By the time that I arrived, in 1971, my father and
mother had decided to name me after this great radical
revolutionary. In my first fifteen years or so I did not
fully understand the significance or the honour of having
the name Luther. To me it was a rather silly, embarrassing middle name. The only person that I really had ever
heard of with this name was 'Lex Luther', the bald baddy
in *Superman*, so I kept quiet. Over the years a few people
picked up on it and I earned an array of nicknames
including Luther Vandross, Luther Blisset, Loofa and
even Lucifer for which I was sorely tempted to deal
out a direct punch to the head. However, turning the
other cheek probably served better in bringing my point
across! Today I'm very proud of my middle name and
have a big picture of Martin Luther King mounted on my
living-room wall with his famous 'I have a dream' speech
as an inspiration.

I am the eldest son of Garth and Gill Hewitt and at the
time of my birth my father was an Anglican curate. As far as
I can make out through pictures, old albums and hearsay,
he was a hippy, guitar-wielding, harmonica-holding, Maidstone curate! In 1972 he decided to go into his music
ministry full time and became a gospel singer. I grew up
in the world of gospel music and in 1973, at the ripe old age
of two, I attended my first Greenbelt festival. Greenbelt is a

long-running Christian-orientated music and arts festival. For the last twenty-five years it has been situated in different fields in Northamptonshire, England and has run for four days over the August bank-holiday weekend. There is more to Greenbelt than just music and arts. There is always a wealth of fantastic Christian speakers and the whole event has a social-justice flavour.

Greenbelt festivals have had a dramatic effect on my life. This was particularly brought home to me as I stood watching mainstage at Greenbelt 98, the twenty-fifth-year celebration. Martin Joseph accompanied by a stage full of familiar Greenbelt faces sang the famous U2 song, 'I still haven't found what I'm looking for'. It was a moment of pause and reflection in appreciation of twenty-five years; not only of the festival, but the family that had grown up within it. The faces on stage with Martin were so familiar, each forming part of the family that we 'Greenbelt kids' had grown up in and learnt to love. Faces had come and gone but there was a core that remained to give us identity in many ways. I have been to twenty-two of the twenty-five Greenbelt years, and have been raised not only on the music of Greenbelt but also on the array of dynamic speakers. It is perhaps a different experience for the Greenbelt kids because the festival has literally been our lives; every single year from before we can remember, Greenbelt has been a part of us.

It was exciting being a Greenbelt kid. As children we were in awe of everything, but as time went on we developed a niche, our own groups of friends. Greenbelt had become our family. Greenbelt was a tribe of people concerned with often different issues than those tackled in most Sunday services. Craig Burrows who works with street children in the Philippines said that he grew up with 'Greenbelt Theology'. Well, such a thing may exist in the very fact that Greenbelt is a place where people have been able to thrash out many different social and theological issues which are often swept under the carpet in other Christian value systems. It has been radical and on the edge.

Greenbelt has never professed to have all the answers but it has not been afraid to ask ethical questions that offend many right-wing Christians. Controversial it has been, yet solid, underlying, exploratory spirituality has guided and steered it. It has attracted a number of non-Christians and some non-Christian bands too, to the horror of extremists. Yet it is very inclusive and this sets it apart from many of the other Christian festivals. Greenbelt encouraged me to think, to be concerned about the rest of the world, to challenge my Western thinking, materialism and doctrine. It has also given me a sense of community for which I am particularly appreciative. I still carry Greenbelt seminar tapes around with me to this day – speakers like James Jones, one of my personal favourites, and others like Jim Wallis, Dave Batstone, John Bell, Elias Chacour, John Smith and many more.

Looking at it from a South African point of view, there have been some 'legends' at Greenbelt, namely: Rev. Frank Chikane (anti-apartheid activist), Caesar Molebatsi (Youth With A Mission, Soweto: radio presenter and now famous talk-show host), Ladysmith Black Mambazo (legendary Zulu choir) and Frank Shayi (Scripture Union). I remember one year having the honour of chatting with Frank Chikane and I was so excited that I felt like I wanted to salute him with a clenched fist singing *Nkosi Sikelele*; fortunately, I didn't!

Greenbelt put into perspective for me the feeling of life being a spiritual journey with much being revealed to us about God along the way, in the hardships and the joys that life deals out. It encourages people not to look for the easy answers, the fall-over-at-the-front-and-everything-will-be-all-right mentality, but rather to ask questions. Challenge yourself enough and you may just see a bit more of God's colourful and exciting plan unfold.

During the last few years Greenbelt became for me a place to meet people with similar concerns and to chat and share experiences. This year I was fortunate enough to be able to exchange ideas with people from brilliant organisations like Casa Alianza, an organisation working with street children in Guatemala and Honduras; the Streetchildren's Consortium, a networking organisation for those working with street children; as well as with the Railway Children, a British project for homeless youth. Being able to chat with such people gives fieldworkers like myself encouragement, strength and new ideas.

Greenbelt will change shape in 1999 by splitting into two events. The first is a similar, smaller, more focused event at Cheltenham Racecourse in July and the other is a youth-based event. As it changes I thank God for all that Greenbelt is, from the aging social hippies to the young radicals, the intellectuals, the musicians, the artists, the performing artists; in fact, everybody. I hope that a new, young, social-activist thinking will be developed and nurtured as the festival continues. It is time for us young folk to carry the torch that our parents lit and encourage the Christian community to embrace issues of social justice and politics. We are strong enough now. It is time for us to take up our responsibilities and stand up for the rights of our brothers and sisters around the world; there are plenty of us.

My father's ministry continued and I remember clearly getting our first video recorder in about 1977 to record him on TV as he was presenting the show *Pop Gospel*. I was so excited. My father appeared with a co-presenter called Bernie and together they sported hairstyles and clothes that today would be illegal and in some countries would command torture or imprisonment!

I grew up in Ealing, London, until the age of ten and those were the happiest, most secure days of my childhood. Throughout my childhood I was excessively into my pastimes. I used to give my hobbies my 100 per cent attention and by the age of nine had shaved my head and was devoted to the pop band Madness. I dreamt of having a pair of DMs and constantly tried to push my mum into buying some for me. I wanted a grade two skinhead and my mum would only allow grade four! I was deeply impressed by the punks and skinheads at the end of my road, at the bus stop outside Pitshanger Lane Library (who I think with hindsight were always drinking alcohol and sniffing glue). I used to try to speak like them and my mum would threaten to send me to elocution lessons.

In those early school years I had what I count as a huge blessing from the Lord. I was put into North Ealing Primary and Middle School, a highly multiracial school with each class consisting of children from many different backgrounds. To me, people having different skin colour and different cultural backgrounds was the norm and I thank God for this experience at such an early age. I loved those days. I knew who I was – I was Thomas and my world was small. We had strong camaraderie amongst our friends and it was then that I became fascinated with other cultures. I particularly loved visiting my Indian and Pakistani friends because whenever they opened the door the food that was being cooked would send the most wonderful rich smells wafting out. I would inhale deeply to soak up the aroma; it was great. As a young boy I was always treated very well by the parents of my cross-cultural and international friends, always feeling at home with and welcomed by them, and I found it fascinating that people could come from such diverse home environments.

We are a very close family and since my brother Ben and I have been able to walk and talk we have been companions. He is a year and a half younger than me and is still my greatest friend. I probably have no one in this world that I am closer to than Ben even to this day. We have shared life together, sharing friends, sharing bedrooms, riding BMXs, skateboarding and surfing together. We are very close and have always had a great relationship with each other.

I have a sister called Abi who is six years younger than me. I am also very close to her and she is a very supportive sister. As kids we were always close; she had to put up with three brothers which made her tough. She always managed to stand on her own, though, and although we now live at opposite ends of the world we remain in contact all the time. Abi has visited me on a number of occasions in South Africa.

My youngest brother is called Joe and at the time of writing he is 18 years old and attending University College of St Mark and St John, Plymouth. Joe and I are very similar, not only in looks but in character as well. Whenever I am home we spend our entire time joking with each other, irritating each other and beating each other up – he is great.

When I was ten years old my parents told me that we were going to leave Ealing. We were going to live in a place called Guildford.

'Is it still in London?' I asked and when my mother replied that it was not I remember feeling worried that I was losing part of my identity. I felt like I was losing my secure base. However, kids bounce back quickly and after a time I stopped missing my friends too much and got stuck in with trying to make a niche in Guildford.

Going to school in Guildford was not so friendly and somehow the kids were different. They had two things that the kids of Ealing didn't have, first, lots of money and, second, lots of sarcasm. The jokes and banter were strangely different. In Ealing we laughed and joked together but in Guildford we laughed at each other and put each other down.

I did, however, enjoy my secondary school years at Guildford County School although my interests were never the same as anyone else's. I was the only person into hip-hop music when I first started there and later I was one of about two people into skateboarding in the whole of Guildford. This statistic later changed dramatically and, as I mentioned before, I was certainly the only one into surfing in the area. I was able to maintain this 'going against the flow' which helped greatly in shaping my identity. I was used to having to pursue my interests on my own.

My closest friends were often outside of school; indeed my two lifelong friends who I consider like brothers, Kristen Meadows and Steve Bewes, were from Chessington and London respectively. These guys were my real friends and still are today. Kristen and I often shared very different hobbies but remained best friends with one mutual interest as teenagers – girls! Steve and I shared many of the same hobbies and enjoyed music together. Steve would often start a new hobby, and then introduce it to me. I would then become a fanatic about this interest, giving it my undivided attention. These two have both been a real encouragement to me as well as a great laugh to be mates with. They have both been out to South Africa to visit as we will see later.

At the age of fifteen I became heavily involved in skateboarding. It was about the time that skateboards made the progression from skinny 'banana boards' into fat, kick-tailed, brightly designed, mean machines. Between the ages of sixteen and eighteen I wasted a lot of time, achieved mediocre A levels and was restless. At the time, skateboarders were starting to get into drugs and I too started looking for my excitement in this area. Fortunately, God had another plan; it is what I call my 'blessing in disguise'. When I was seventeen years old, one summer's day I was visiting the local skateboard ramp, a 'half-pipe' about ten feet high. I attempted to do a fairly easy trick that I didn't pay much attention to and as I came back down to land I 'wiped out', landing on my shoulder with whiplash in my back. I had to shuffle home and lie flat on my back for quite some time. Even after a fairly unproductive operation the pain has never completely subsided, although it is slightly better these days due to keeping fit and strengthening the muscles around the injury. However, I was never able to skateboard again without pain. God used this opportunity to take me out of the skateboarding scene and this forced me to review my life.

God is a great, merciful God and my back problem only seemed to flare up with sports involving jarring on the ground and so, thankfully, I was able to continue my surfing. Indeed it became a vehicle for God to use to expose me to my vocation.

As a boy I had been taught the fundamental elements of Christianity. I had attended Sunday school and had a realisation of being a child of God from a very early age. I knew that God should be the central point of my life. However, I never seemed to fit into the youth programmes at our church, St Saviour's in Guildford. I realise that it was my fault, not theirs! St Saviours church is very supportive of me now for which I am very grateful, but I did give them an uphill struggle as a lad! I clearly remember constantly being reprimanded by the verger for drawing surfing pictures all over my service sheet and I wonder how the vicar, David Bracewell, put up with my brother and me continually giggling at the back. I did enjoy boys' club led by a man called Alan Mansfield as it appealed to the slightly tougher local kids in the parish and was more of a laugh with lots of games and indoor soccer.

As I got older I stopped going to boys' club and continued going to what was called 'Wayfarers'. This happened after the evening service on Sundays. I had a good friend called Matt Hawdon and together we used to cause untold grief for the really nice people who ran Wayfarers. We sat at the back ridiculing the speakers, cracking jokes, sniggering during open prayer and generally making a noise. We would embarrass our visiting friends by explaining that it was compulsory for them to pray aloud during open prayer,

and generally just fooled around. I think that I will take this
opportunity to apologise to all my former Wayfarer leaders
especially Dave and Marion Peters who are just about the
nicest, most friendly, welcoming and supportive couple you
could imagine. Sorry for making your lives miserable at
Wayfarers!

In the late seventies my father was asked to go to Haiti by
Tear Fund. This tour was to reshape the direction of his
ministry from gospel-singing evangelist to Christian activist, fighting for social justice and human rights. He did this
by encouraging people in developing countries and helping
to tell the stories of victims of poverty and injustice to the
rest of the world, to try and be a voice for the voiceless.

The Amos Trust was formed in 1985 by my father and
other concerned Christians to support my father's music
ministry, as many of the countries that he visited could not
afford even the basic expenses. Since then Amos Trust has
grown and is now much more than this. It has partners and
supports projects in South Africa, the Philippines, Uganda,
Palestine-Israel and Nicaragua. It still maintains its commitment to social justice and to linking arms with the
oppressed around the world.

I was uneasy about my life at this time and I thank God
that I never took hard drugs because I know that they could
have potentially ruined me (bearing in mind how much I
devote myself to my interests!). I am a person who needs
purpose in my life, we probably all are, but I did not feel
fulfilled or have any peace at this stage. My father realised
this and in the midst of my negative period he arranged for
me to accompany him on an Amos Trust trip to South
Africa in the summer of 1990 which had been arranged by
the Anglican Church and the South African Council of
Churches.

South Africa – it sounded so exciting. I knew about the
political and social horrors there. My father had educated
me as to who Nelson Mandela was and what the apartheid

system was doing in South Africa. I was also a member of anti-apartheid groups in London. The film *Cry Freedom* about the banned South African journalist, Donald Woods, and his friendship with black, anti-apartheid activist Steve Biko had a huge effect on my life and inspired me to take an interest in South Africa. It was a film that I continued to watch again and again over the coming years. I did not realise that one day I would be living in East London, the area in which it was based.

My first recollection of Africa is the view from the plane as my father and I flew in to the airport in Cape Town. As we approached the runway I was looking out of my window, shocked as we flew a few feet over one of Cape Town's squatter camps. It was an awesome sight, a mass of tiny shacks, a real shantytown. I could see people wrapped in blankets carrying buckets of water on their heads. It was obviously cold outside. The shack settlement seemed endless, a mass of tin broken only by dirt roads, dust blowing furiously in the wind. It was reminiscent of what I had seen on TV in the news bulletins, and in *Cry Freedom*. I couldn't believe it; I was about to land in the world of apartheid. I was now going to see it all first-hand. As I drove through Cape Town the thing that really struck me first was how there were Coca-Cola adverts everywhere. However, since then I have come to realise that however remote an area in Africa, Coca-Cola always seems to be there.

On my first evening in South Africa we attended a church service and towards the end they sang the famous song that was the anthem of the struggle, '*Nkosi Sikelela iAfrika*'. It was a spiritual moment for me, yet I did not know why. I did not know that God was changing my life from that moment on.

My first impressions of actually being inside a black township were very memorable. The first squatter camp that I visited was called Khayelitsha, one of the biggest in the country. It was a cold, wet and windy day making the

dirt roads extremely slippery and muddy. As we drove
through the area on our way to visit a clinic, I saw row
upon row of shacks knocked together with tin, scrap metal
and scrap wood. These were people's homes. It was amazing. The people were poorly dressed in inadequate clothing
for the cold but they huddled together, sharing blankets.
One of the first things that I noticed was how many children
were running around playing. They were everywhere. None
of them had shoes; most just had a pair of shorts and an old
T-shirt. The rain had turned some parts of the township
into mudbaths and children carrying buckets of water
negotiated their way through the mud.

The people were very friendly which to be honest was
something that I had not expected. I had thought that they
would be angry, taking apartheid and how the whites had
oppressed the blacks into consideration. We had gone to
observe the living conditions in the townships before meeting some of the residents who would give us first-hand
accounts of living in apartheid South Africa. Everyone was
very friendly to my father and myself despite our white
skins. I was confused by this.

Children would watch us carefully and when they felt it
was safe they would wave. On one occasion I noticed a
group of children smiling and waving. Naively I leaned out
of the window to take a photograph. As I did this, they all
jumped up and ran away, screaming. My action with my
camera had looked like I was going to shoot them with a
gun. A black woman called Lulu who was one of the
organisers of the tour quickly got out of the car and called
them back, explaining probably that I was a brainless fool
from overseas! They came back and I took a picture of them
and we parted with smiles and waves. A reaction like theirs
comes only from experience and it suddenly dawned on me
that these were children growing up as victims of the
oppressive apartheid regime.

Within a few minutes of leaving the township we were

driving through a rich white area. What a contrast! It was luxurious, peaceful, clean, beautiful – something was very, very wrong. I sat in the car open-mouthed. I was stunned and upset and even though my father had seen it before he too was visibly upset and angry.

We moved around the country visiting townships and talking with and listening to the communities to try and get as much of an overview as possible of the apartheid problem. My father sang and encouraged the people and gathered as much information as possible to tell those back in the UK. It was an education for me. One area we went to was Bloemfontein in the Orange Free State, heart of the Afrikaaner area. The black community here suffered terribly at the hands of the white farmers. One morning my father and I were accompanying some black community members on a trip to town on our way to attend a meeting with the community. We went into the bank with them as well as other places. The town nearly came to a standstill. White people literally stopped in their tracks as they saw us striding confidently together up the street. It was too much for them. You could see them becoming angry, their eyes were like daggers. Our black friends were laughing; they thought it was great fun. I thought the whites in the streets were going to damage their necks for they were trying so hard to turn and stare at us!

We visited schools, refugee camps and African National Congress (ANC) rallies. I have never felt such a sense of excitement and people power than that of an ANC rally that we visited in the Kwa-Zulu Natal area. It was overwhelming. We had been invited by the tour organisers and my father played some songs of encouragement and freedom and the community, packed into a huge hall, told stories and engaged in songs and chants of freedom. They would shout '*Viva* Comrade Mandela – *Viva*!' and '*Viva* MK – *Viva*!' ('MK' stands for Umkhonto weSizwe – the military wing of the ANC during the anti-apartheid struggle.) Their list was endless as they paid tribute to freedom fighters, activists and anti-apartheid movements. After my father finished singing they even shouted '*Viva* Comrade Garth!' The people were so warm – I loved them.

We then moved on to an area of the Eden Valley in Kwa-Zulu Natal called Imbali. This was an ANC area which was devastated by Inkatha fighting. The Inkatha Freedom Party (IFP) is a Zulu-based political party headed by Chief Buthelezi in the Natal area of South Africa. Historically it has always been opposed to the ANC. Inkatha were more sympathetic to the old government, toeing their line, and as a consequence were not so harassed by that regime. They did not fight for freedom in the struggle, and in Kwa-Zulu Natal there is still fierce ANC/IFP fighting. The ANC would view them as 'sell-outs'.

We met with a group called the Imbali Support Group where we first heard stories of people who had had family members murdered, their houses burnt down and who were literally on the run. They also told of a 'third force', namely the police, who they believed were supporting Inkatha to destroy the ANC in the area. The idea of a third force was fiercely denied by the government and whites in general at the time but a few years later all the evidence came out and the 'third force' was exposed. The Imbali Support Group had known this but nobody listened to them.

They told us that if Inkatha knew that we were in the house with them they would try to kill us. It was at that moment that I wondered about the wisdom of placing me in all my whiteness in the seat by the window! However, I was not about to say anything. That day I met activists and revolutionaries who inspired me greatly. These were people going against the flow, who dared to challenge the system and were paying the price. I often wonder whatever became of the Imbali Support Group and its dedicated members.

We then went to visit a refugee camp which comprised a mixture of Mozambican refugees who had fled the civil war in their country at the time and South Africans fleeing political violence. It was fascinating to actually meet and be able to talk openly with the refugees.

After meeting members of the communities of Soweto, Khayelitsha, Bloemfontein, Kwa-Zulu Natal and Swaziland, we went to Mozambique to meet with the Anglican Bishop of Lebombo, Dinis Singulane. This man had a great effect on me as we stayed with him. He showed me street children living by his house. The whole street was just full of these kids. They literally lined it; there were hundreds of them. I was devastated. Never before had I seen children actually living on the streets. Most of them were escaping the violence and civil war in Mozambique. It was an upsetting moment, an awakening for me. It put many things in my life into perspective as to what was really important. The memory of that day lodged very deeply in my heart and was in fact going to change the direction of my life. Bishop Dinis was involved in helping the kids and his servant attitude towards them made an impact on me, perhaps even giving me some sort of role model.

The South Africa 1990 trip planted many seeds in my heart, not least of all the desire to work with street children. God would keep this seed stored for a few years while he prepared me for the job. I did not realise then just how close to my heart God had placed the children of the streets. I had met people who were radical, who had real goals. They were determined people who often worked in most oppressive of situations; they were dedicated to fighting for their brothers and sisters and they saw Jesus in others. They were not afraid to go against the flow, yet at the same time they were people not really that different from myself or anyone else. But they were willing to be used by God, willing to do God's plan and willing to die for the struggle. They were real people, they were activists – but then, wasn't Jesus? Didn't he go against the flow and wasn't he radical and outspoken? The first time that Jesus describes his own ministry he

quotes from Isaiah 61 and adds a bit from Isaiah 58 in
Luke 4: 18–19:

> The Spirit of the Lord is on me,
> because he has anointed me
> to preach good news to the poor.
> He has sent me to proclaim freedom for the prisoners
> and recovery of sight for the blind,
> to release the oppressed,
> to proclaim the year of the Lord's favour.

This is radical and this is Jesus describing his own ministry.
As followers of Jesus this should also be our manifesto.

When I arrived back in the UK although I was the same
on the surface my South African trip had changed me
forever. In 1991 I visited South Africa again briefly to keep
up my links with the country but it was more of a surfing
holiday. I stayed with my good friends Brian and Pauline
Cape whose hospitality was instrumental in my return to
South Africa in 1992.

On 27 September 1992 I boarded a plane to South Africa
to stay indefinitely. I had given up my job as a runner for a
video-editing company in Soho, packed my bag and surfboard and embarked on the journey of my life. I was
twenty-one years old. Brian Cape had offered me a job
when I was in South Africa in 1991 and I decided to take
him up on the offer. I lived with his family in Johannesburg
for about eight months, which was great. I was yearning,
however, to get stuck in to serving the community in some
way but I did not know how.

I decided to leave Jo'burg and visit friends in the Eastern
Cape. It was there that I took up an offer to visit East
London for a surfing competition, where I met a guy called
Brad Cuff. Brad offered me a place to stay at his Queens-
bury Bay home while I looked for something worthwhile to
get involved with. Apart from being a fantastic point break

for surfing, Queensbury Bay is a wonderful quiet beach where I was able to pray often and really ask God to show me what he wanted to do with my life.

In East London I started to befriend the street children who used to live by the main beachfront. I quickly became known and trusted by them. I wanted to find out if there were any organisations working with them so I asked a local pastor in the area. He told me about a little place in the township called Isaiah 58. I did not have transport at the time so I asked Brad if he would come to visit this place for street children in Duncan Village, East London. Brad, myself and two others went to visit and before long I was a volunteer worker there.

I stayed in East London for the next five and a half years. I became involved with the Amos Trust who supported me to work at the Isaiah 58 Children's Village as project co-ordinator and to serve as one of the board of directors working with the street children of East London. I later joined another organisation for street children in East London called Daily Bread where I was childcare director for over a year. In July 1997 I moved to Durban to work alongside local projects in setting up a team to monitor and work with children at street level to encourage them off the streets.

I am eternally grateful to God for giving me the privilege of seeing South Africa during the apartheid regime; it changed the way I saw the world. I am also very grateful to my father who gently turned my life around through our trip in 1990; his wisdom changed me.

3   A history of pain and unrest

'South Africa is free at last!' These were the words of the new president, Nelson Mandela, after the 1994 elections when the apartheid regime was overthrown and a new coalition government headed by the African National Congress party (ANC) was put into place.

It had indeed been a long devastating struggle of which the facts are still emerging today through the findings of the Truth and Reconciliation Commission. The TRC was set up to investigate all abuses of human rights throughout the apartheid years. The extent of human rights abuse is terrifying as real-life, harrowing situations are brought to light, the agony of the oppressed is finally made public and the perpetrators are exposed.

If I was to go into real detail about the history of apartheid I would need another book or perhaps ten! I do, however, want to try and paint a picture of the horrors of apartheid as it also has direct bearing on the plight of street children today.

The Union of South Africa that had been formed early in the twentieth century recognised the rights of whites but not those of blacks. The laws and taxes at the time were specifically designed to make Africans leave their land. The ANC was formed with the specific aim of bringing all Africans together as one people and to defend their rights and freedom.

Oppression, however, worsened during the first half of the century and in 1948 the National party won the elections and officially implemented the policy of apartheid which meant completely separate development for the

1. Weybridge Christian
   fellowship

2. Dr. Mary's friends

3. Virginia Water

4. Daughter going to

5. Work with Jon
   ~~fro~~

Should Malcolm say a
prayer after vote of thanks?

Old habits
die hard.

Two sides to S Africa.
Street children parents
Great deal to be done.
dedicated people
500,000 children a Durban
street — Aids crisis

Street Educators Team
shelters
Streetwise for boys
Youth to, drink — girls
Rehabilitation/ Crisis
centre for
children

different race groups. Many oppressive laws were put into place – resulting in blacks being underpaid, receiving inferior education, and having to carry passbooks everywhere. This led to strikes, boycotts and defiance campaigns led by liberation movements such as the ANC, the Pan Africanist Congress (PAC), the United Democratic Front (UDF), and the South African Communist Party (SACP).

The PAC and ANC embarked on an anti-pass campaign and on 21 March 1960 a group of peaceful PAC protesters gathered, without passes, at police stations to be arrested. At Sharpeville the police opened fire on the unarmed crowd, killing 69 and wounding 186 people, many of whom were shot in the back. The Sharpeville massacre, perpetrated by the South African police, brought a decade of peaceful protests to an end and paved the way for armed struggle. The ANC and the PAC were banned soon after the massacre, and a decision was made by these organisations to launch the armed struggle.

In 1961 the military wing of the ANC was formed, called *Umkhonto weSizwe* (MK), which means 'spear of the nation', to 'hit back by all the means within our power in defence of our people, our future and our freedom'. In 1963 the leaders of MK, including Nelson Mandela, were arrested and charged with attempting to cause a violent revolution. They were all sentenced to life imprisonment. By this time the UN general assembly had called for economic and diplomatic sanctions on South Africa.

The might and power of the evil apartheid laws manifested themselves in the creation of townships and in the daily life of the black community. Townships emerged from a policy of Separate Development which was a way of shoving blacks into small government-allotted areas, tucked away out of sight. Of course, in comparison, the white areas were extremely affluent and houses were normally equipped with an array of luxuries – servants, swimming pools, carefully landscaped gardens and Mercedes Benz parked in the drive.

Black townships were the downside of apartheid. Instead of the luxuries, the blacks had to contend with tiny tin shacks, overcrowding, and the absence of the most basic amenities. Laws were enforced to ensure that blacks received an inferior education, were barred from land-ownership and allowed only basic jobs; there was no hope of ever climbing the economic ladder from within the townships. Coupled with the threat of violence from the police for stepping out of line, the townships offered a depressing existence.

The townships often had no running water or toilet facilities and in the squatter camps as many as twelve people would live together in one shack. With a mixture of the breakdown of family values, abject poverty and high un-employment the townships became dangerous places. Life was really tough for the kids in the overcrowded townships. Violence was ever present, political violence was all around them; they were living in the armed struggle. Children grew up witnessing horrific incidents which would often leave them traumatised. Violence came in many forms and was often perpetrated by the vicious South African police or the army.

Local violence was also prevalent. 'Necklacing' – a form of mob injustice whereby a tyre was thrown around the neck of the victim, they were doused with petrol and then burned to death – was a commonplace punishment for informers. The burning of their property, often with them inside, was also a familiar sight.

Violence increased within townships, spurred on by al-cohol, and stabbings and shootings became the norm. There was no real policing and community action was sometimes the only way to sort out problems. One 8-year-old boy called Xolela, who I have worked with over my time in South Africa, was in the house with only his father when a group of men came in and shot his father dead in front of him. He ran, and kept on running, ending up on the streets.

Of course, the violence in the townships was overshadowed by appalling political violence carried out by the apartheid government against anyone who spoke or acted against the fascist regime. Children grew up in fear, familiar with seeing the police and army launching into the area heavy-handedly in their armoured 'Caspars', beating up activists and often murdering them. Many children witnessed violent forced removal by the police and army and many watched their friends and families arrested and thrown into the police trucks. Some children experienced the inside of prison cells and were indeed tortured themselves.

The 1970s saw apartheid grow and in 1973 the ultra-right-wing, Nazi-style, Afrikaaner Movement (AWB) was formed. In 1976, however, came the incident that many have said signalled the end of apartheid. Schoolchildren in Soweto demonstrated peacefully against the government making Afrikaans the medium of instruction. Afrikaans was seen by the black community as the language of the oppressor. The police opened fire on the children, killing young Hector Peterson and at least three others. The uprising spread to other parts of the country and left over a thousand people dead, mostly killed by police. Most of the dead were teenagers. The Soweto uprising changed international thinking and also mobilised the youth, many of whom joined MK.

Protests continued and the government embarked on eliminating anyone they considered a threat. In 1977 Steve Biko, leader of the Black Consciousness movement, was murdered by police while in detention. The film *Cry Freedom* was written about Steve Biko and his friendship with newspaper editor Donald Woods. He had used his brilliant mind and had promoted Black Consciousness globally through his writing, speeches and actions. Naturally his death infuriated his community but it also caused an international outrage because he was viewed as way ahead of his time and a natural leader and hero of the black people. The TRC is at present dealing with the security police responsible for his death who, twenty-two years after they killed him, may face charges for the murder of Steve Biko.

I was in East London in 1997 when Nelson Mandela unveiled a statue of Biko in the main street of the town outside the town hall. Many political leaders were there from all parties, and a few notable persons from overseas like Richard Branson and Peter Gabriel. Gabriel had written a song to honour Biko a number of years earlier. The unveiling was a moving occasion as thousands congregated to commemorate this great thinker and revolutionary.

The 1980s were bloody years and the people pushed the struggle in all areas. White hit-squads murdered prominent black leaders. There were a few reforms, but they were weak and changed nothing. In 1985 the freedom fighters called on local communities to make the black townships ungovernable by destroying black local authorities, which were seen as puppets of the system. Troops and police moved in and engaged in constant battles with the comrades, who were often youths armed with stones and petrol bombs. As resistance mounted the regime became more vicious and between 1986 and 1990 a national state of emergency was declared.

Apart from some notable radicals, the white population supported the apartheid regime. However, the government censored the media and the news bulletins were so doctored that the general public did not have the full picture. Most white people had never set foot inside a township, yet they felt they knew what was best for the blacks.

In 1990, however, due to mass pressure from the people and outside sanctions, the government was forced to un-ban the ANC, PAC, Communist Party and other organisations.

Nelson Mandela was released on 11 February of the same year after spending twenty-seven years as a prisoner of the evil system. Apartheid was collapsing, and the government was forced into reforms. In 1992 F.W. de Klerk called for a whites-only referendum on whether to continue negotiations with Mandela and those parties fighting for freedom about reforming the apartheid system and the possibility of the first free and fair elections – 62.6% said, 'YES!' Negotiations began.

Life for the average black South African had not changed yet. Indeed, one lad that I know, Nkosinathi, was present at the 1992 Bisho massacre. Troops of the then leader of the so-called Republic of Ciskei, a declared black homeland puppet dependent on the white regime, opened fire on a peaceful ANC rally at the Bisho stadium. Nkosinathi was part of the chaos as the crowd ran for cover under a hail of bullets and he watched people drop as they were shot dead. He was twelve years old at the time.

In the run-up to the 1994 elections, right-wingers still continued efforts to destabilise the country. On 10 April 1993 Chris Hani, Secretary General of the Communist Party and former MK Chief of Staff, was murdered by men linked with the Conservative Party, a right-wing white party.

I remember the 1994 national elections, the first free elections in the history of South Africa. It was a wonderful day, freedom had come. I was able to take part in the day as a peace monitor at one of the main polling stations in East London. People queued for hours wearing their best clothes, some had made dresses and bought suits for the occasion. I will never forget the joy in the faces of black South Africans voting for the first time in their lives. It is an experience I cherish greatly. It was an extremely peaceful day, which came as a shock to most whites, many of whom had stocked up with food and rations, expecting to have to go into hiding. The ANC unanimously won the election and so headed up the new coalition government with ANC leader Nelson Mandela as President of South Africa. Mandela and the new government set about trying to redress the extensive damage of apartheid – a job that will take decades.

Since the elections, things have improved but at a much slower rate than was anticipated. Attitudes have not changed greatly within the white community, rather they have taken to excessive whinging, often termed 'white wine'. Whites still control the majority of business despite rigorous affirmative action.

The black community still, for the most part, live in the same conditions as before, in the same townships. There are many development projects under way to try and address the massive social problems but the legacy of apartheid has left deep wounds. City centres have become much blacker as people try and move from the townships. In turn the whites have retreated into their suburbs alongside a very few new wealthy blacks. One disturbing aspect is the rise of classism within the black community with a new 'middle class' with little compassion for their brothers and sisters in the squatter areas. The majority still live in poverty. Freedom has arrived but the struggle for liberation from economic apartheid, poverty and AIDS continues and will do so for a long time.

There are estimated to be some 100 million street children worldwide today. The phenomenon of street children is not a new one. It is, however, a problem that can be tackled, with the right systems in place in each city and town that has street children. People often ask me, 'Where do these children come from? Are they all orphans?' As simple as such questions sound, they are an important place to start in the quest to understand the mechanics of the problem.

As a result of the apartheid regime, urban South Africa was left with horrific and vast problems. Rural South Africa was also affected greatly but it was predominantly urban conditions that gave rise to the street children phenomenon. Townships became chaotic; the strange mixture of oppressive laws and lawlessness had a devastating effect on people. A marginalised people lived in poverty with huge unemployment numbers. No significant government measures were ever taken to improve the townships.

The only contact that whites had with the black community was to use them in a servant capacity as maids, petrol attendants, gardeners, factory workers; all the menial jobs. Very few whites ever went into a township to see how the blacks lived, yet the blacks saw how whites lived in luxury every day. Many white families still have live-in black maids working for them. These maids usually stay in servants' quarters away from the main house, yet they wait upon the white family, usually for very little pay. These women know everything about the way white people live, from what they eat for supper to how they like their trousers pressed. These women live away from their families simply to be able to support them. I've never met a white family that has spent any considerable amount of time at their maid's house in the township. Most would not even know how to find it.

Children living in the squatter camps became prime candidates to become street children for a number of reasons. First, and most obviously, they were living in poverty, which means many families had no source of income and not enough food. This is a reason in itself to take to the clean streets to beg for money. Sometimes children were even sent by their parents to beg and bring back what they could for the families to eat.

In addition, children were not growing up in proper family structures. Their fathers were working miles away in the mines, or their mothers worked in the white suburbs with only a few days off a month. This was destroying their culture of community alongside strong families. The family was often seen as the nucleus of African culture. The apartheid system was actually turning certain parts of society into a shambles and children were obviously the hardest hit.

Children became familiar with sjamboks (heavy whips), AK47s, pistols and other weapons. Informers were killed with bricks, stones or sticks. These images have a great effect on the mind of a child and I wasn't surprised one day on the streets of East London when the street children decided to take revenge on the man who had been raping them. It was like a scene from one of Michael Buerk's news reports during the apartheid years. They surrounded the man and began stoning him with large rocks. I saw each rock hit his head and body with unforgettable cracks and thuds. The man staggered, trying to protect himself, but the more blows that he received the more his body became weak, unco-ordinated and confused. He was weak at the knees, going down. The children, aged between nine and seventeen, had had enough and this was the only way they knew of taking action.

I had to protect the man by jumping in and stopping the kids. I knew that if I did not do this the man would die. I cannot say that I enjoyed saving the man because I hated what this man had done to the children and was fully aware of the hollowness of my statement to the children as I urged them to deal with him through the proper channels, the police. Unfortunately, they knew this was as good as letting him go.

Many of the children that I have worked with often witnessed necklacing. One girl that I spoke to, Mandisa, said that she had been there when a man had been burned to death in this manner. At the age of eleven, she had been in the crowd watching as the comrades killed an informer. She had been scared on that occasion, but had seen necklacings before. A girl called Lulama told me of how she had been at school when a witchdoctor had run on to the property and into the playground with an angry mob following her. The community mob then threw a tyre around her neck, poured on petrol and burned her to death. She burnt to death in front of the children in their playground.

In oppressed communities where there is little hope, people often look for ways of escaping the pain and one way is to 'drink' the pain away. Alcohol abuse became rife in the squatter camps and in turn brought a whole wealth of other problems. The children always seemed to be the ones who suffered most, whether personally as victims or by seeing events that no child should have to witness.

Township life had two major effects on the street children situation of the 1990s. First, children grew up as victims of violence, thus finding it difficult to adjust to becoming adults and then themselves often falling into the trap of violence and abuse. In other words, a wounded nation grew up and manifested itself in vast social problems, lawlessness and lack of respect for life. Second, township life had a detrimental effect on the day-to-day existence of some children, forcing them to flee their townships and run to the city streets.

Today the situation has not greatly changed because, whereas government violence is no longer existent, the townships still remain as extremely dangerous places. In some areas there is still political violence especially in the Kwa-Zulu Natal area where there is fierce ANC and In-katha fighting. The mixture of alcohol abuse, political violence, social violence, unemployment, complete lack of recreational facilities, lack of adequate schooling, poverty, lack of sufficient welfare support, overcrowded shacks and squatter camps leaves the township children living in fear today.

South Africa has the highest rape rate in the world and its children are the most vulnerable. In the projects that I've worked at I have found almost all of the girls that I have come into contact with have been raped at least once in their life. In fact, I'm quite amazed at the way children and indeed women are constantly harassed openly by black South African men whether it be at home, in the streets, on the beach, or while shopping. South African women and children have to put up with harassment and abuse daily.

Within the townships and squatter camps most girls become sexually active very early on, but rape is often their first sexual experience. The South African rape rate is directly related, I believe, to this attitude of domination over women which I feel may be a direct manifestation of the damage caused by growing up in such horrific circumstances.

To be more specific about what forces children out on to the streets, I believe we can put these children into different categories as to how they arrive on the streets. The first group includes those who are lost, abandoned or orphaned. These children have no alternative. Children often get lost or split from their families in big, busy African cities or on the beaches. This often happens over Christmas and the New Year as it is now traditional for the black community to swamp the city beaches over this period. This is ironic, as during apartheid they were not allowed to use these 'white' beaches. Some of these children are very young and so reuniting them with their parents is often very difficult. The danger, of course, is that they are instantly vulnerable to street life as well as to just about any other abuse possible. Sometimes the police or a concerned citizen will take these children to a shelter, but the problem is that the longer they stay away from their real home the greater the risk of them learning the ways of the streets or of the children living at the shelter. Being lost can be an instant introduction into a whole world from which the child was previously safe.

Other children who are literally dumped into street life are those who have been abandoned by their parents and indeed the categories of lost and abandoned children overlap tremendously. Often, with such poverty in the township, parents may simply abandon their kids on the city streets thus relieving the pressure at home. These children, dazed and bewildered, wander around dejectedly until they start to find a begging patch or perhaps become friends with other children of the streets.

Often when a child is abandoned it will be left by its parents with a grandmother or relative who is either too old or not equipped to look after a child. This is a story that I've heard hundreds of times. It always sounds pretty much the same: 'My mother left and went to Johannesburg. I do not know my father. I was left at my grandmother's. She has no money and can't look after me.' There are many grandmothers struggling to bring up abandoned children in South Africa. Many of these kids will end up as street children.

There is also a newer reason for children running to the streets. This reason is AIDS. There are so many new AIDS orphans and, as I will explain in the next chapter, it is a phenomenon that is going to increase dramatically.

The second group of children includes those who are sent by their parents and those who flee their home areas due to poverty, violence or sexual abuse. Some families are so poor that parents send their children to the streets to beg for money and often tell them not to come back unless they have money. Other parents work in the streets themselves, taking their young children with them who, from an early age, become very streetwise. The majority of children, however, arrive on the streets by fleeing from their local areas. There are many different reasons which drive children to search for a better life on the streets and often it is a mixture of these that finally makes them become a street child.

Poverty is a word that covers many aspects. Often the children are hungry in the townships, they do not have enough money for clothes or to go to school. Even though education is supposed to be free in South Africa, the children still have to pay school fees at all schools, they still have to buy school uniform and books if they want to attend. Some families are so poor that this is just not possible.

Many children suffer from boredom and neglect at home. With a lack of recreational facilities, and simply nothing to do, it is not long before the children start looking further afield. Some children commit crimes within their townships and run away to the streets to escape punishment.

We have seen that the children in the townships are very vulnerable to sexual and physical abuse and this is a major factor in children running to the streets; they simply have to get away. Some have to escape abusive parents, others from members of their extended family who are sexually abusing them, and some need to simply escape the everyday scenes of violence to which they are subjected. Children run to the streets due to the alcohol situation at home which often results in them being beaten up. Sometimes it is just too much, watching their fathers beat their mothers or their mother beating up their little brothers and sisters when they are drunk.

The problem is that although these children may feel that they are running to a better life, the abuses to which they have been subjected in the townships are reinforced on the streets and sometimes life just continues to get worse. It is as if these children are caught in a downward spiral; there seems to be no way out. Children jump out of the frying pan and into the fire.

4   Street life

Three loud cracks rang out. I opened my eyes and sat up quickly – that was gunfire! Again, two more shots rang out. I leapt over to the open window. From seventeen floors up, I could clearly see a man lying on the ground. A police car pulled up and then sped off in pursuit. I legged it, putting on a pair of shorts, a jersey and some flip-flops. Grabbing my camera, I jumped in the lift. I wanted to see what was going on.

There was blood on the ground, cars had been sprayed with bullet holes as the fighters had taken refuge behind them; it was like the movies. A man lay bleeding, he wasn't that serious though. Another man lay inside the casino entrance, more serious but not critical. It was a western right outside my window. Yet for the street children who swarmed the scene, it was right under their noses; they saw it all.

I heard 'There's Tom' ring out from the kids and soon I had the whole story. It had been a gang battle. The kids didn't seem shocked, for they had seen it all before. They just hovered around the scene with their glue bottles, much to the annoyance of the swarms of police that had just arrived. The police were mostly white and Indian and before too long they had lost patience with the street children, who in all fairness were not actually doing anything wrong. Just the sight of the street children seemed to antagonise the South African police and I had heard rumours from the kids of physical abuse dealt to them by police officers.

One of the boys, who had apparently endured long-standing tension from one particular police officer at the scene, got into an argument with a drunken reveller who started pushing the kid around. The policeman ignored the reveller and started pointing his finger in the face of the lad. The situation got more heated and the policeman punched him and then again, three times. I couldn't believe it. In front of a huge crowd he was physically abusing the boy. All the other police just looked on. I kept shooting film, capturing exactly what was happening. The other street kids gathered around and started to hurl verbal insults at the police – they were obviously quite familiar with this type of abuse. They kept on looking at me, saying, 'Yeah – keep shooting.'

I did so. The kids stood by me, thrilled that the abuse wasn't going unnoticed. One child, aged about thirteen, stood by me as I took photos. His eyes were fixed on the fight and he was really excited that we had a picture. Every time the camera flashed he shouted, 'Yes!' He got so carried away that when I paused from shooting he said to me, 'Here, I'll do it', as if he was helping me out! He said it so confidently, as if he was a photographer by day and a street kid by night. I laughed about it for a long time afterwards.

Soon the police were trying to disperse the children by running at them with tear-gas containers in their hands. The way they did it, though, was so antagonistic that it was like whipping up a riot. The street children backed off to a safe distance but for no reason at all a policeman ran at them with a growling, fierce police dog. This is not a new tactic; a large percentage of street children have scars to show from being attacked in this manner.

I was capturing all this on film when a policeman came up to me and said, 'Who are you and where do you come from?'

I said nothing. He said, 'You can't shoot photos.'

I said, 'Why not? This is a public area.'

He said it was a crime scene and they were still trying to assess the area. I said, 'Fine, I'll stop.'

He knew that I had damaging evidence on film and said, 'Where is your press card?'

I told him I wasn't from the press and that there was no law stopping people taking pictures in a public area. He called another police officer over and said, 'Put him in the vehicle.'

They took me and put me in the back of a squad car. Inside the car I noticed that it was impossible to get out. I sat there, watching what was happening. The police wouldn't speak to me. They kept me in the car for ages to try and scare me. Meanwhile they beat up the boy who was already bleeding from being punched. Four burly police officers picked him up. He was kicking and screaming. One of the police officers said, 'Throw him in the back of the van with the dogs.'

I thought to myself that a few moments ago I had been lying in bed listening to gunfire, and it was now a street kid and myself who had had nothing to do with the shoot-out who were the only ones that had been arrested. I tried to think, 'How did I end up in here?' As I did I laughed. However, I did not laugh for long because I was thinking about what that poor lad was going through. I knew that they could not charge me with anything because there were many witnesses. But I also knew that if they were capable of human rights abuses against children they were also capable of making up some charge against me to cover up their actions.

The police officer came back to the car and ordered me to give him my camera. He took it and went to his colleagues; again they left me for ages. He then ripped out the film and screwed it up. He kept it, came back to me and gave me my empty camera saying, 'You can go.'

He had destroyed the evidence. I realised that the police didn't enforce the laws here; they made them. I kept quiet and walked back into the crowd where the children were really pleased to see me. The fact that I had been arrested was no big deal to them, but they seemed to acknowledge that I was willing to stand up for them. I felt that we had bonded that night. I also realised that the kids were living in constant danger on the streets.

When a child enters the realms of street life, that child does not always intend to stay on the streets. Many children get into the habit of coming to town every day to beg and then go home, often begging for their parents and then returning to them late at night with loose change to feed the family with; they are often seen as breadwinners. These children are what I term as 'type 1 street children'. They don't live on the streets. They have a home but poverty forces them to beg during the day. These are children at risk. But there are many I know who like to live like this. They see street life every day but do not get sucked into it, often because they have some kind of security (however small) to hold on to at home. Some see street life and the effect it has on other children and are scared to stay on the streets at night, however bad things may be at home.

More often than not these type 1 street children do eventually become what I term as 'type 2' street children – full-time street children. This usually occurs because they hook up with friends or make new friends on the streets and feel secure enough in these gangs or groups. I prefer the word 'groups' because 'gangs' automatically conjures up the image of hard youth with intent to do crime. I believe street children get sucked into a life of crime rather than choosing it.

Life on the streets starts with the typical images that many of us have seen on TV or in the newspapers. Children sleeping rough on the streets, huddled together for warmth, sharing a blanket if they are lucky, begging for loose change from passers-by, often being totally ignored by the general public. It is a familiar sight to see children scratching around in the rubbish bins. Sometimes the children are so small that to reach the rubbish at the bottom of the bin they are literally upside-down and almost fully submerged. On city street corners, groups of kids gather, playing, fighting sometimes or just sitting quietly watching the world go by, almost always sniffing glue.

The deeper, more damaging aspects of street life seem to hit the kids all at once and are always intertwined. The children become targets of physical and sexual abuse. Ninety per cent of street boys according to a survey done in East London, South Africa, have been sexually abused on the streets and I do not know a street girl who has not been raped. They are sitting ducks and older street kids or street people often rape the children who live and are therefore vulnerable in the same area. No one wants to be raped so they usually take a beating in the process. Girls get gang-raped by other street dwellers often as do the little boys. These attacks will often happen at night when the children try and find somewhere to sleep.

A group of street girls that I knew were violently gang-raped at a little makeshift home they had made under a skateboard ramp in the beachfront area. Desperate kids used to cram themselves in there at night until one night a gang of men attacked the place and gang-raped the girls and the small boys. When I reported this to the Child Protection Unit (CPU) in East London a certain sergeant who will remain nameless simply laughed and said to me, 'These children ask for it – I'm not going to open a case for them.'

In the end I forced him to take the details but nothing was ever done about it.

The children soon find out that a way to earn money to survive is through prostitution. The children are in demand and on entering a 'group', the older children who are by now hardened prostitutes start the younger ones off, usually taking their money at the end in exchange for a bit of food, protection and a place in the group. Children as young as eleven wait on known street corners to be picked up. They sell themselves for as little as ten rand (one pound) and even less depending on the job. Their clientele vary in background but I have noticed that the majority of these people come from the white community and are often middle-class men driving up-market cars. My theory for this is that with apartheid in South Africa the whites often thought of the blacks as subhuman, almost animal. So it is therefore easier for a white paedophile to live with himself after abusing a black child than it would be if the child was white, because he may not feel that the child is worth anything; it's not a real child in his eyes.

In Durban the profile of child prostitution is very different. The girls who run on to the streets often do not sleep on the streets for more than a few days because they get sucked in to what I term the 'flats' lifestyle where they live as prostitutes in low-cost accommodation. These girls can be as young as twelve and they earn enough to pay the rent, feed themselves and to pay for a few extras. These girls are very hard to identify as they keep themselves very clean and dress well to attract customers. Some girls work in organised escort agencies particularly serving the visiting sailors, and often have their accommodation paid for. For many of these girls there is no way out of prostitution because they have no education and will never find a job. They feel that at least with prostitution they can survive and don't have to live literally on the streets.

The boys also turn to prostitution, particularly the younger ones; and they perform sexual favours to men who pick them up in cars or other men on the streets. These boys are often taken and sodomised by the abusers; some of the children can be as young as six or seven.

I knew a young black reporter at the *Daily Dispatch* newspaper in East London. You may remember from Richard Attenborough's film *Cry Freedom* that the *Daily Dispatch* was where Donald Woods was the editor back in the 1970s. The reporter Simphiwe Piliso was interested in the work of Isaiah 58, the project I was working at.

However, when he started to hear the stories from the streets he decided he wanted to do a story about child prostitution. Simphiwe agreed not to use their real names and I weighed up the pros and cons of coverage. The authorities needed a wake-up call because despite requests from us they seemed to deny the problem. This was echoed when Simphiwe phoned the CPU chief and asked, 'What happens about the child prostitution in East London?'

The policeman replied, 'There is no prostitution in East London.' With this I took Simphiwe down to the street for an informal chat with the girls. We spoke to Felicia and she, trusting me implicitly, told him everything that had happened. He could not believe it. He decided to write an article and expose this situation. However, what we didn't want was a mass public crackdown throwing these kids into jail. What we did want was that the abusers be targeted and a public recognition of the problem so that we could then try and deal with the children through projects. Unfortunately this did not happen.

One of the problems of child prostitution is that the children often do not realise the extent of self-damage and in a strange way they learn how to survive for a short time on the streets through this. Children living on the streets have a high risk of catching AIDS. Prostitution, abuse, casual sex with their peers and lack of medical care makes them instant targets. The AIDS statistics for the Kwa-Zulu Natal (KZN) area are frightening. It is estimated that 32 per cent of all pregnant mothers are HIV-positive. Some hospitals report up to 50 per cent. Seventy-five people become infected every minute in South Africa. One in three of the KZN population are estimated to be HIV-positive. Other hospitals have claimed that 80 per cent of the corpses in the morgue are HIV-positive. In the month of April 1997 alone there were 5,973 reported new cases of infection in the KZN area.

What does this mean for the street children? Recently in a

city in South Africa fifteen street children were tested and eleven were HIV-positive. We are living on a time bomb because of the window period for HIV turning to fully blown AIDS. The dying has not really started in full force but it will not be long now. Unless something is done, the street children are just going to start dying anonymously.

By the year 2004 it is expected that there will be 2.5 million AIDS orphans – in other words, those whose parents have died of AIDS – in South Africa. About five hundred thousand of these will be in the KZN area. The AIDS orphans will almost certainly mean that the number of street children is going to swell dramatically. I cannot begin to imagine what this will mean for a city like Durban where there are already hundreds of street children. If the issue is not properly addressed, street children will simply die and have their places filled by other AIDS orphans who will in turn just die. The outlook is bleak.

There are many sad stories of children barely surviving on the streets and one girl who has shown me the oppressiveness of living there is Felicia. Felicia's life story is a complete tragedy. She arrived on the streets in 1994 at the age of fourteen, a very pretty girl with the most lovely soft eyes. I found her huddled with the small street boys one cold night and asked her where she was from. To my surprise she answered me in perfect English. She lied to me and told me that she was from King Williams Town. However, I later realised why she lied: she did not want to be taken home. She came from an area of the township called Parkridge, close to the Isaiah 58 site where she had stayed with her grandmother and relatives. Her mother had abandoned her and she was always quick to remind me that her mother did not love her. At her uncle's house she was being raped regularly by her uncle and his friends; by coming to the streets she was escaping them.

Within a couple of months she had met up with another street girl called Nomsa, a seasoned child prostitute who was also fourteen at the time. Nomsa had been on the streets since the age of eleven and had herself escaped one of the notoriously dangerous shack settlements called Ziphunzana. Nomsa soon taught Felicia how to make a meagre living through prostitution and they became best friends. At the age of fourteen, living a life of prostitution destroys a child physically and mentally. Not surprisingly, the way that both girls attempted to cope with it was by sniffing benzine to dull the horrifically degrading reality. Each night they would wait on a certain street corner, always high on benzine, waiting for cars to pull up to take them to the public toilets on the beachfront for men to have sex with them. Their prostitution would support the rest of the members of their group who would also use the girls for sex. Their sexuality was worth nothing and soon Felicia was the most insecure girl I knew. She literally thought that she was worthless, a piece of rubbish. Felicia was also constantly raped on the streets by older street dwellers; it was ironic because the very reason she came to the streets was to escape from rape. She was trapped; she had nowhere else to go.

Felicia used to come to church with UK volunteer Anna Joseph and myself. After a while we could see that she trusted us and desperately wanted help. Felicia made a commitment to the Lord and we used to pray with her every day. She studied Scripture Union Bible notes and I noticed something interesting; when it came to choosing notes she always wanted the notes designed for slightly younger children. Also, when watching television, her favourites were the cartoons and children's TV. It seemed as though the suppressed child in her was trying to come out. We bent the rules and found a place for her with some Christian friends of mine; however, this did not work out. They just did not have the time for her, much as they had wanted to. Anna and some local Christian folk took her in. She stayed with them happily but it was midterm so we could not get her into school and were concerned that she did not have enough to do during the day. Amazingly, the projects would not take her because they felt that she was too streetwise although she was only fifteen at the time. When Anna returned home, Felicia panicked and ran away; she could not cope with having to live with another family. She ran back to the streets and straight back into her old lifestyle.

Tragically, to this day Felicia and Nomsa continue in the lifestyle of prostitution and benzine, yet it is now visibly taking its toll on them both. Felicia has sadly lost her good looks. Her face now looks worn; she is covered in scars and looks like a much older woman. She is very thin, possibly having contracted HIV/AIDS and is dependent on benzine all of the time. When high, she now becomes wild as if telling the world that she has lost hope. Although she is a shadow of her former self, sometimes when we chat her brilliant eyes light up penetrating through her tired face. She will always remind me that she still loves God and prays to him every night. She seems to hold on to the Lord from somewhere deep inside. I know that her faith in the most harsh of conditions is cherished by the very heart of God.

One of the fundamental elements of street life that almost always goes alongside the prostitution is sniffing glue or benzine. Durban's street children sniff a highly toxic, addictive glue that they become dependent upon – it has long-term, destructive effects. This glue actually starts to paralyse them after a while. The kids start to lose co-ordination in their legs and eventually cannot walk at all. This is a slowly reversible process if caught early enough but we still have not established the depths of the long-term effects. In East London the children do not sniff glue. They sniff benzine, a paint stripper which appears to be slightly less addictive than glue but has damaging long-term effects. Hard drugs are not really part of street life for these kids because they simply cannot afford them and are therefore not interested. Most of the children smoke marijuana because it is so cheap in South Africa.

In East London the children sniff benzine for the same reasons the children in Durban sniff glue: to escape from the depressing life they are being sucked into. It also helps to take away the hunger pains on the streets. The children pour benzine on to a rag or on to their clothing and inhale it through their mouths. It has a twofold effect alongside the prostitution. First, it helps the children escape from the reality of their traumatic lifestyle, the degrading of their bodies, the destruction of their dignity. It also helps them to lose their inhibitions to enable them to partake in the sexual acts demanded by their clients. Benzine is cheap and easily obtainable in many stores. One bottle can be shared among many and anyone looking eighteen or over can buy it. There are young people on the streets in East London who have sniffed benzine for so long that by the age of eighteen they are already walking like an elderly person and lacking bodily control and co-ordination. Their minds are very damaged and it is unlikely that they will ever be functional socially again – it is very sad to see.

All newcomers to the streets are vulnerable to the temptation of glue or benzine; it makes life a little bit more bearable. I am not sure why the children of East London do not sniff glue, or the children of Durban do not sniff benzine, but I think it is to do with what is available in each town and force of habit. I have seen kids as young as five sniffing. Often these little kids sniffing glue endear themselves to the general public. When they are high they amuse passers-by as they dance or are hyperactive. In Durban all the street kids sniff glue. You will see children every day inhaling through their mouths from plastic milkshake bottles. The children do this all day, day in, day out. Local street-workers say that the children develop sores from the glue on their bodies and, if you press around the edges of the sores, glue seeps out. Some local people say that it is this glue that keeps the children on the streets and stops them going to the local shelters. I believe that this is partly true.

Joe Walker, an Amos volunteer who has been out to work for me twice, was talking to two traumatised street kids one night in Durban. Both were about twelve years old. Joe noticed that their hair was stuck together in big lumps. He asked them what happened and they told him of an incident that had occurred that day where the police had ordered them off the beach for swimming in the sea (in a designated swimming area). The policemen then poured their glue on their heads. The boys were repeatedly punched in the face by the police and then told to punch each other. Incidents like this seem all too common in South Africa, yet they traumatise children.

I remember one morning when I was phoned by one of the workers at the Daily Bread Project and told that there was a boy who had been arrested for breaking into a car and that he had asked for me. I arrived to see that the boy was dripping wet. The police had caught him and had been holding him in the cells; they had also soaked him for no reason from head to foot with cold water. It was a cold East London winter's day. The boy was shivering, frozen, and was offered no relief from the heavy soaked clothes that hung on him.

Police in South Africa have often been seen to ill-treat the street children. Tear gas is used to disperse the kids. Sometimes when they are sleeping they are awoken by tear gas being sprayed in their eyes as police move them on. I've also seen police lunge at groups of street kids with tear gas. The police like to egg each other on when they are doing this. They are also very quick to use police dogs if children resist arrest. I have witnessed countless injuries to children after being attacked by police dogs. This leaves the children traumatised as well as physically scarred. Police send police dogs after street kids even if they are just suspects to a crime, even with no evidence of their involvement at all. It's as if the police have the power to prescribe the punishment of being mauled even before any evidence has been collected. I know three children who have been shot at by the police. Two of the boys were in court for a petty crime, but they were so fearful of going to prison that they escaped from the court and as they were running away the police shot at them. Who are they to think that they can prescribe the death penalty on these kids! The other boy was Boy-Boy who was used as a look-out at an unarmed robbery and the police shot him through the leg as he ran away. One can argue that he was involved in a serious crime but I feel to shoot at him like that was unnecessary.

Another police trick is to load up all the kids from a certain area, then to drive them out into the bush in the middle of the night and drop them each on their own about 2 or 3 km apart from each other without telling them where they are. They leave them petrified, having to find their way back from the middle of nowhere. This is a particularly cruel way to treat innocent children often as young as six or seven. The police are trying to deal with the problem of street children from an inhumane point of view, not thinking of them as children but as worthless pests to society.

One night I found two tiny children, aged approximately two and three, shivering, trying to get to sleep. They were outside a casino in down-town Durban in the notoriously dangerous Point Road area. I was talking with two concerned passers-by when two policemen came by and refused to do anything. They said they wouldn't touch them. One of the policemen said, 'These kids need a good hiding to get them home, but when we beat them the newspaper always shouts abuse and gives the police a bad name. If I beat a child he won't come back here in a hurry.'

Perhaps that explains the mentality.

Seeing children living on the streets often makes us, the general public, say, 'It's so sad', or 'Where are their

parents?', or 'How can these poor children live like this?'
These are all good compassionate reactions but the reality of
street life should make people say, 'This is horrific – we must
do something', or 'How can we as society allow these
atrocities to happen?' or 'We must join together and fight
against this and not give up until every child is cared for.' An
impossible goal, some might say – so what! A vision doesn't
have to be achievable instantly. Many visionaries die because
their dreams are too radical for society or because they go
against the norms of society, and so put their lives at risk.
However, if others pick up their vision, pick up the torch and
run with it, there is hope. God plants vision into people but
the completion of his dreams is not limited to the vision-
bearer. He or she is simply a messenger or activist. The best
and probably the most radical example of this is Jesus.

In most cities where street kids live, the public only
become aware of their situation when the kids start to
threaten business or tourism. Indeed in Durban the street
kids are the prime components of the so-called urban decay
blamed for the increase in violence and homelessness and
the decrease in business and tourism in the down-town area.
On one level I can see their point. The city needs to thrive
financially, must be safe and must have the capacity to
attract tourism. One down-town shopkeeper decided to deal
with the problem in a militant style and adopted a zero-
tolerance approach to street kids hanging out near his shop.
He would chase and threaten the kids. Recently the shop
was burned down, totally gutted inside, allegedly by these
very kids. Whether it was the kids or not, the approach was
wrong because it dehumanised the children and treated
them as outcasts.

Street children invariably get caught up in a life of petty
crime; breaking in to cars, houses, shops and sometimes
robbing people. Sooner or later the police will arrest them
and they will be sent to prison. Nelson Mandela made an
order that children were not to be kept in prison. Plain and

simply, this has not been adhered to. I have been inside East London Prison where I met with many children, most of whom I knew from the streets. They were living in a supposed youth wing of the prison; however, I saw inmates in their late twenties. The conditions are basic but the big problem is that sexual abuse is rife. All children in prison are used by other inmates for sex. Street children sit in prison while they are awaiting trial. Occasionally children get sent to reform school but have to sit in prison, often for months, until the case is tried. Every child in prison is forced to join a prison gang and have gang numbers tattooed on their bodies. The gangs use the children for sex on the inside and later for crime on the outside. Children are put in prison for petty crimes alongside murderers and rapists and child abusers, and when they finally get out they are hardened criminals, abused and often ready to abuse.

AIDS is rife within the prisons and sticking children in prison awaiting trial for petty crimes is like pronouncing the death sentence on them. Sibongile was a really outgoing, happy child on the streets who did not take glue or benzine. However, when he was fourteen the police arrested him and he sat in prison for six months. When he came out his character had changed completely; he was withdrawn, had a stutter, and could not look me in the eye for months. He had no confidence, he was a different child. I took Sibongile to one of the projects where I was working and he is now recovering.

Once a child reaches fifteen or sixteen on the streets having lived there for some years, it is very difficult to break the streets in them. Up to this stage the kids have mostly been involved in petty crime. However, from now on, life starts getting tougher. They start losing that sweet innocent face, ideal for begging, and become young adults, at least physically. The boys move on from simply being the abused, often to being the abuser. Almost all of the older street boys have forced sex upon younger girls or sometimes little boys. They have grown up in a lawless society which teaches them that they are not important. If they do not even love themselves it's hard to imagine them understanding love for others. Years of 'street schooling' begin to bear rotten fruit.

With his bullish build and bodily scars, Sinovuyo had an intimidating aura about him; he was tough. He was not tall but his natural, well-built, thick frame gave him power. He was not afraid of anything or anyone – he ruled every patch he entered. For most street dwellers his name struck fear in their hearts. Sinovuyo had grown up on the streets from a small boy, indeed he had lived by their rules for many years. The street children projects had not been able to deal with Sinovuyo in his young years and when he was that little bit older they did not want him, he frightened them.

From an early age he learnt survival, so much so that by the age of sixteen he had etched out a comfortable existence controlling one of the groups of street children. He never had to beg, his income came from the girls who were involved in prostitution. He was supported so well by these faithful and probably more petrified girls that he was able to afford to drink and smoke dope every night. He never took benzine and I think that this was because he was clever enough to see that those who did were not able to control themselves or command power. Sinovuyo set up a shack in the bushes that was impossible to access unless you knew the pathways. He stayed there with about ten other children and chose which girl to sleep with.

Sinovuyo did have a compassionate streak in him but as time went on the streets were overtaking him. The more he felt he controlled the streets, they in fact controlled him. He had been your typical street kid; mild mannered and cute at an early age but toughened with time and experience. As a young boy he was breaking into cars and houses but by the age of about fourteen he had started to move on. One of the local prostitutes let him share her room at the local brothel and by the age of sixteen he was raping young girls and had already committed his first murder.

Sinovuyo had reached the top of his profession – he ruled the streets – yet obviously it was less than fulfilling and for some reason he became attached to me. We would often sit and chat together and I realised that he was searching for Jesus. We would go to church together and he would often bring kids who had just arrived on the streets to me. We even prayed together on some occasions. Sinovuyo knew that his life was not on the right track, yet it was so difficult for him to change. He looked up to me, always wanted to help me and be around me; he desperately wanted to feel that we were friends. I tried hard to introduce him to Jesus Christ yet, as much as I tried, as soon as I was not there he would be involved in something wrong. I think by being close to me, part of him felt that he could move on to more power, the world of flats, cars and a bit of money. Another distant part of him really needed a role model, a father to encourage, appreciate and love him.

I remember one night very well where Sinovuyo's presence helped me in a potentially dangerous situation. I was working with the kids on the streets one day with Amos volunteer, Joe Walker. We happened to be outside the notorious Beach, a known brothel and hotel in East London, with a group of kids that we worked with daily. We were almost finished and Joe went to the car; some of the children called me back to point out to me a man who had been abusing them. At that moment the man realised that we were watching him. He came over to me and drew a knife. Obviously he viewed me as a threat – clearly I knew too much now. He pushed the knife in the vicinity of my throat and face, waving it threateningly but, as he did this, after a few tense seconds passed where I remained motionless, he suddenly seemed to lose his nerve. Sinovuyo was standing by, watching the scene very closely. This seemed to worry the man and he suddenly retreated and in fact ran away.

I think that it was actually Sinovuyo's presence and not my weak attempt to remain completely calm that actually saved me from more serious trouble that day. Of course God was there with me the whole time and I feel that he really protected me. The kids all laughed afterwards but it was no big deal to them and I must admit that I laughed more out of nervousness and to keep face. When I got back to the car I said to Joe excitedly, 'Did you see that?'

'See what?' he replied!

Sinovuyo did indeed protect me on the streets but the worse that he got the more I as a Christian started taking a stand against his activities. Despite the input we gave him spiritually, he seemed addicted to increasing his power on the streets and was a danger to society. He was a mess, a pure product of the streets. Afraid of nobody, he lived by the knife. Time was running out for him. He was in and out of prison and he had made many enemies, although most of them were too scared to do anything. He once got stabbed in a fight where he was outnumbered and for a short time he had a limp and couldn't move one of his legs properly – this was a relief to many but he seemed to know how to fight against it. He stole a bicycle and cycled everywhere and in no time he was completely strong again and getting tougher. Every time he went to prison he would do press-ups and other body building exercises and would come out bigger still.

By mid 1997 he was also playing power games with me. It seemed like he had to conquer everyone in order to feel good about himself, he knew only how to dominate. I started to get worried because he would try and intimidate me if I did not have any food or something nice for him. It was, however, imperative not to show him my fear because as soon as I did it would mean that I was in the streets on his terms, and this was not a good witness to the other kids as to them Sinovuyo stood for the evil, violent way.

We still used to sit and chat in the car but although he

would always listen to me, the Christian interest seemed to be confined to the car; as soon as he got out it was back to his life of violence. In the car he would pick many little arguments in a friendly manner but it felt like he really needed to win those arguments to test me to see if I would give in to him.

Although I did suspect him of a beachfront murder I did not realise that he was already responsible for about three murders and maybe more at that time. He had allegedly killed his brother, a drinker on the beachfront, and a young girl who he had first raped. He had started drinking heavily at night and this seemed to be when he felt his most invincible. I met him a few times when he was drunk and he really was terrifying, he would get out his huge knife and show it to me closely. I used to wonder how many people had died from its sharp blade. At around this time he even went to a witchdoctor to get a *muti* (medicine) which supposedly made him powerful and invincible against the police. No matter how bad you are, when you make a deal with Satan he will always let you down. He had tricked Sinovuyo into an evil life with false expectations.

His reign of terror on the streets continued and I remember praying that the police would pick him up. I knew they would not yet. God's intervention seemed to be the only thing that would stop him. One night Sinovuyo lifted some loose change from an old homeless man who was asleep. Another drunk 25-year-old man visiting East London from the Transkei saw this and shouted, 'Hey, boy! Leave the old man.'

The term 'boy' infuriated Sinovuyo who got up, enraged, ran to the man and stabbed him deeply in the heart. The man collapsed and died. Sinovuyo ran like an athlete and nobody dreamt of trying to stop him.

I had an agonising decision to make: whether or not to inform the police as to his whereabouts. I was not worried about him going to prison; my main concern was that something would go wrong, as it invariably seemed to do. He would escape from prison or court or the police would not have enough evidence, and he would be back on the streets. I was not really worried that he would kill me – which was a possibility because he trusted me and had little concept of right and wrong – but that he would make it impossible for me to work with the kids on the streets, by manipulating and intimidating them.

He came to see me and I told him that the man was dead. This had absolutely no impact on him. I spoke about Jesus Christ. I told Sinovuyo that he was involved in evil; again he listened but the boy in him had been overtaken by evil. I must admit that he remained very friendly to me but I knew that his days as king of the streets were numbered and he needed to be stopped and punished.

How I wished that I had in fact handed him in, although I know he would not have agreed to go. One month later he forced sexual advances upon an 18-year-old girl on the dance floor at the Queens Hotel in East London. She refused him and a fight broke out; he drew his familiar knife and stabbed her viciously in the chest under the arm – she died instantly. One of the boys who had witnessed more than one of his murders said that just before he killed someone he would growl deeply from his chest like a dog and then pounce; it sounded almost demonic. Nobody present tried to stop Sinovuyo as he walked out of the club.

Finally, however, the police were hunting for him. I was devastated by what he had done and I handed over as much information as I could to the police. The police officer in charge was a really friendly guy and told me that they were going to find him. He was wanted in connection with eight murders. Sinovuyo remained at large for about a month until the police received a tip-off as to his whereabouts. He had ventured down to the beachfront area again. The police searched but in vain; it seemed that he would evade the police once again. Then out of the blue they spotted him and gave chase. He just vanished into nowhere. The police were totally stunned and were about to give up when one of them looked under a parked car in the area – there he was. He bolted and they drew their guns and warned him that they would shoot him. He turned around, looked at the guns, looked around, saw the game was up and stopped. At last he was off the streets.

Sinovuyo now sits in Fort Glamorgan Prison in East London, South Africa, for his entire life or until he escapes again. I wouldn't like to say which I think is more likely! He is paying for a life of terror and the day he escapes is the day East London has to watch out. He became engrossed in evil, but despite the string of murders and all the other horrific acts he committed I can't help but acknowledge that it was in fact a life on the streets that turned him into what society would label as a monster. He was a victim of the streets. I saw good characteristics in him in the early days. He had to fight for his survival as a boy and he never stopped fighting, always running, always on the edge. He was in many respects a tragic figure destined for disaster – a pure product of the streets.

It is vital to get kids off the streets as soon as possible because, although all things are possible through God, sometimes the damage and effects on the kids' lives is almost irreversible. What is the future for a street child if left on the streets? Well, perhaps they will be murdered or maimed through street violence, or they will destroy themselves on glue and end up dead, or they will contract HIV/AIDS and ultimately die; this is perhaps the biggest threat to the kids. Others will end up serving long prison sentences for crimes committed in the streets. Nobody really survives a life on the streets.

I receive messages from Sinovuyo from other kids released from prison; he wants me to help him and I will, but not in the way that he thinks. Even if I wanted to help him there is nothing that I could do to get him out, and that is right because he is a threat to society and needs to deal with the consequences of his choices. I will, however, go and visit him and remind him of that wonderful good news of a man called Jesus Christ, indeed, the Son of God who was sent by his Father so that sinners like Sinovuyo and myself might be able to receive forgiveness and even more; eternal life with the Father in paradise. Although he will have to live with what he has done for the rest of his life, through the Lord's unending mercy he may one day find his peace. I have a feeling that Sinovuyo may be ready to listen to God now.

It is the stories of people like Sinovuyo and Felicia that remind us that something needs to be done to try and rescue these children from street life. Realistically, what can be done? Often people say to me that it's such a big problem that is it really worth trying. After all, for every child taken off the streets there seems to be another very soon to replace it. The real key to trying to help the situation is to realise that each child is a child of God, precious in its own right and in fact, as far as I am concerned, if I battled all my life and was only able to rescue and give a future and a hope to one child it would have been worth it.

In my opinion working with street children is a twofold venture. The first part of the work is what I term as street work; actually entering the realm of the streets, becoming a listening ear, a voice for the kids and of course encouraging them off the streets. But 'where to?' you may ask. Well, that is where the second part of the work comes in and that is the residential projects; the children's homes or shelters. It is vital that the two aspects – the street work and the projects – work together as they both depend on each other and, most importantly, effective handling of the problem depends on the two being intertwined.

Sometimes children's lives are permanently changed by street work on its own; especially those whose family situation is such that they do not need the project and simply need to be returned home. Street work is really emergency work, if you like, the street rescue service. It is the groundwork to relocating the children to the projects or, as I mentioned, back to their parents. Successful street work will never encourage children into the streets nor will it make life so easy for the street kids that they feel that they do not need the projects; this would merely encourage the Sinovuyo scenario.

The basic aim of the work is to encourage the kids off the streets and to do this the team or individual needs to form a base friendship of trust with the kids. Although there may be times when one feels that to buy some food for them would really be helpful, it is important not to start supporting their street lifestyle. It is, however, important as a street-worker to be a listening ear, a stable influence, an encouragement to them as individuals, reminding them of their worth as human beings and as God's children. As a Christian myself I also try to introduce the option of holding on to the love and promises of Jesus Christ and, if the children so desire, I pray with them, study the Bible and just generally chat about the great hope. It is really important to be a good witness to the kids and show them how to love because you may be the only person in their lives ever to do that. Street children are ignored by society, so much time needs to be spent standing with the kids as a voice for them, campaigning and standing up for their rights in places like court and against such abuses as child prostitution, police brutality and victimisation and abuse from the general public. The kids encounter endless problems on the streets. Street-workers often become involved in mediating in scuffles and disputes on the streets as well as endlessly driving kids to and from the local hospital to have wounds sewn up.

Later on I will explain a few ideas that I have for expanding street work. Street work can provide breaks from the hardships of street life in the form of fun, outings and games. In East London we would often take the children out to the beach or to local farms, and every Christmas we had a special party on the streets at night in an empty carpark where we bought a big bucket of fried chicken and played dance music on the car stereo. The kids loved it, they would eat and then dance.

Being a Christian working on the streets, I see children every day who not only need the basic physical necessities of life but also are desperately in need of knowing and feeling the love of Jesus. In our 'chats' on the streets we often talk about praying and trusting in God. One of the major differences between street children and other South African black children and indeed most Western children is that they are not embarrassed by church or Christianity. In fact, they often embrace it even if they have no idea of how to apply it in their lives. I have found it amazing that if you ask any street kid 'Do you love Jesus?' the answer will invariably be 'Yes, of course' and it is not seen as uncool at all. This really makes a big difference because it automatically means that they are interested in finding out more about the love of God. Christianity is never forced on them but we make it known that there is a road available to them with Christ; of course, if they wish to pursue this we are always ready to help them.

I remember one boy called Siphiwo who was about fourteen when I met him on the streets. He was going down very quickly, sinking into a world of sniffing benzine and drinking cheap wine. The combination made him wild. He was in and out of prison, usually because he made such a noise while drunk that the police always seemed to find him. One night he was stabbing one of the girls on the street. I saw this and dived into the fight to try and protect her. I grabbed the knife and pulled him away, which was not too difficult in view of his condition. We calmed him down and checked the girl, who was not seriously wounded. The next day I went and found him before he started sniffing; he was sober and we started chatting. He really wanted to change his life so I told him about Jesus. We sat and talked and I asked him if he would like this Jesus in his life. He said yes, so we prayed. I did not realise how much he needed God right at that point, but a couple of days later he was arrested as a suspect in a car-breaking case and thrown into prison. I had bought him a Bible in Xhosa and he really had made a genuine commitment. I went to the prison one day with a local community worker and good friend of mine called Patrick Lottering. Patrick was doing sports with the inmates and I saw Siphiwo. He smiled and told me that he had not forgotten about that night. It was a really exciting moment because there was a ray of hope in the midst of the dismal prison conditions; it had meant that the night we prayed had really meant something to him and had led to comfort and support for him in prison. About one year later he was released and I happened across him one day in the township. He told me that he was still a Christian and was not on the streets but living with his family – what is more, he wanted a Bible. Kids like Siphiwo have been through tremendous struggle in their short lives and somehow the Bible and the way of Jesus seems to offer them something new, a hope and peace.

The street kids always wanted to come to church with me. It was always an interesting experience, not least the first time we went together. It was a mixed church in the centre of town. Typically, I arrived late and unfortunately there were only seats available right at the side of the front. Our band of filthy, dishevelled, tough-looking kids self-consciously walked to their places, quickly sat down and sank into the seats. The congregation looked up in amazement at the spectacle. It was a little unfortunate, we had not planned to be late but we did not want to leave anyone behind when rounding up the kids. We had not planned to make such a statement! The kids actually handled the service fine and at the end told me that they wanted to come back next week. It was great because the kids started to realise that church was as much for them as the rest of the congregation, and that Christ was not interested in their dirty clothes. The congregation were friendly and the kids felt at home. In South Africa it is culturally correct among the black community to dress up for church in your best suit, often your only suit. This is slightly unfortunate for the street kids who have no nice clothes and you will often hear them saying, 'I want to go to church but I've got no clothes for it.' It is quite a major stumbling-block to them because if they do decide to go to church they will probably feel embarrassed about their attire.

Street children need allies; they need friends and guidance, they need to feel accepted and ultimately they need a way off the streets. Some children are able to go back to their families but for some, due to the home situation, this is impossible. Part of my work on the street is to identify the children, reunite them with their families or come up with a new alternative. This is where the residential care facilities come in and play a vital role in the rehabilitation and rescuing of street children.

This chapter is about real life and real children who suffer daily. There is always the temptation to give up on the children or to say that they are a lost cause. There *is* hope and it comes directly from the great giver of hope himself: Jesus in his sermon on the mount. In Luke 6: 20–2 Jesus says:

> Blessed are you who are poor,
> for yours is the kingdom of God.
> Blessed are you who hunger now,
> for you will be satisfied.
> Blessed are you who weep now,
> for you will laugh.
> Blessed are you when people hate you,
> when they exclude you and insult you
> and reject your name as evil, because of the Son of Man.

Here Jesus highlights the importance of the poor, hungry, sad, the persecuted, the oppressed and the defamed; the street children are prime examples of such people and if Jesus loved them enough to die for them, we should at least be prepared to show love for them.

5 A future and a hope

I remember with fondness my early days at Isaiah 58 Children's Village. Auntie Maggie, the senior housemother mentioned in Chapter 1, had taught the children how to have a day-to-day spiritual relationship with God. When they had no food they literally prayed to the Lord, asking him to supply their needs. The children would get together at about seven o'clock in the evening and would sing worship songs before going into a time of prayer where the children prayed individually but at the same time out loud. Many visitors silently wept as they watched, and often joined in with the Isaiah kids as they prayed to God, their maker, knowing that he loved them so much.

I have never before or after witnessed such faith, with the possible exception of the Aliwal North project, Miracle House, where I found a similar phenomenon. Visitors arrived at Isaiah 58 with the notion of coming to minister spiritually to the children but left feeling that the kids had ministered more to them. Many people including myself were opened up to a new form of spirituality by meeting these children. Never have I felt God's presence as much as during these times of prayer and singing. The children would often simply break down and cry, lying face down, pouring out their hearts. This is a natural, God-ordained spirituality, powerful yet gentle. I laughed as I thought of many of the local Christians sending their pastors on expensive trips overseas to collect a form of spirituality that could apparently only be received from specific pastors and congregations in a city called Toronto. It was ironic that under their very noses God was revealing the real nature of the Holy

Spirit in these forgotten children, yet these churches were too busy raising money to realise. I hope they found what they were looking for and that it lasted, because the Isaiah children had found the true heart of God open and on offer to everybody in a little corner of the township.

Although the importance of proper counselling measures and a social work department within the project is vital, I couldn't help but realise that the Lord was bridging the gap in counselling using the most dynamic counsellor ever – his Holy Spirit. Being part of Isaiah 58 revealed to me many things about the nature of God, but I think that most of all it showed me just how unending God's love and compassion is for the street children and just how much he weeps for them in their suffering.

These spiritual times at Isaiah, which had started long before I arrived, continued right the way through my time there and were great times to refuel and to allow God to teach us how to set up a dynamic programme for the street children of East London.

It was also at this stage that I started to look at the scripture verses of Isaiah 58 itself, particularly where it says in verses 6 and 7:

Is not this the kind of fasting I have chosen:
to loose the chains of injustice,
and untie the cords of the yoke,
to set the oppressed free,
and break every yoke?
Is it not to share your food with the hungry
and to provide the poor wanderer with shelter –
when you see the naked, to clothe them,
and not to turn away from your own flesh and blood?

It was then that I realised that this little place, named after this passage in the Bible, tucked away in one of the townships of East London, South Africa, was a modern-day example of a group of people obeying and understanding God's plea to us to love one another and to actively support and encourage the oppressed.

Isaiah 58 is a unique place, an oasis for under-privileged children, particularly the street children and those who have grown up on the rubbish dumps. To be really effective in the area of working with street children, together with the spiritual aspects one has to remember that the work needs to comprise at least two facets: the street work and a well-run childcare facility. This chapter will particularly focus on the latter.

The project may be run very differently now, with slightly changed aims; however, I do know that it is very successful and many of the original children are still continuing to grow in leaps and bounds. I first visited Isaiah 58 in early 1993 and, as I entered the gates with my friend Brad Cuff and two others, one of the first things that I noticed was how excited the children were to see us. It appeared that they did not get that many visitors and we spent the entire evening playing games, singing songs and chatting to the kids and staff. At that time I did not know how to speak any Xhosa, their language, so relied very much on the language of love.

I remember feeling the magic of the place immediately; the presence of God's spirit was so evident and there was real joy in the hearts and faces of these kids despite having lived with so much struggle and hardship. The children lived in a large tin shack about sixty feet long. Inside there was no real floor, half the wooden beds were broken and there were a few damaged cupboards and wardrobes. At the end of the shack were two beds for the housemothers – local ladies who lived at the project – they also had a little wardrobe for their few belongings. Outside there was a tiny little kitchen and small toilet and shower block – the only two brick buildings. The shower block had only just been completed and was donated by local Christians. The grounds were quite extensive but totally out of control, with wild bush

growing uncontrollably with the exception of a small gar-
den area where the staff and children grew a few vegetables.

I knew from that day that it was a project with great
potential. It needed so much support and yet I could sense
that God had a dynamic plan for it. One of the most
significant aspects of this first encounter with Isaiah 58
was meeting Auntie Maggie. Unbeknown to us at the time,
we were about to form a working partnership that would
stretch over the next three and a half years and a friendship
that would last forever. Although she ruled with an iron fist
(she had to) the children loved her, and she was the 'mother'
and indeed the backbone of Isaiah 58.

With the encouragement of Auntie Maggie I continued to
visit the project about twice a week and often had to borrow
cars from local folk to get there. When these were unavail-
able I used to hitch into the township from town or, if I had
a little bit of money, I would catch the black taxis. I loved
the place, the kids especially. There seemed to be a certain
spirituality about the place and I prayed that God would
make it possible for me to help the project on a more
permanent basis. A few months later I started as Project
Co-ordinator after meetings with Isaiah 58, a local church
and Amos Trust who were going to employ me to work at
the project.

As a team we embarked on trying to build up the project,
raising the standards of living allowing us to cater for more
and more street children. We attempted to address the many
dimensions of childcare that the children had missed out on
through lack of support and lack of staff.

Government involvement

Unfortunately, there are no hard and fast guidelines that
determine how work with street children is to be adminis-
tered. One of the problems is that street children projects

are often judged on the criteria that were stipulated by the government when administering white children's homes, and obviously the problems are very different in terms of the backgrounds of the children. Social workers are given no practical training with street children, so they often misunderstand the needs of street children when applying methods to try and deal with them. The concept of trying to fit the new South Africa into the rules, regulations and structures of the 10 per cent or so that used to rule has frequently proved fruitless and chaotic, especially in the area of welfare. New structures are needed to incorporate the whole community.

The government has tried to tackle the problem of street children to a certain extent, but has not given any serious new guidelines nor has it affirmed any successful initiatives already at work. In a country with such a backlog of social needs, the issue of street kids simply does not seem to be a priority and few people have looked deeply enough into the problem to come out with any guidelines, ideas or even any statistics. Various papers have been issued by the government; some toy with increasing fostering care, others with closing down shelters, others with formalising the working in the area of street children and various different 'shot in the dark' ideas. However, the problem is that there are no real avenues open to creative management, support and rehabilitation of street children and there is very little, if any, money to support street children projects. Those that are supported have outdated 'white' guidelines to adhere to.

Shelters

Shelters (emergency homes) are very difficult to get government funding for, due to the very basic facilities that they offer, and kids who live at these homes often remain living in poverty. By their very nature they are not the answer because they are often located very close to the street area that the children have been living in and therefore never actually take the children out of street life. Shelters can be very positive, however, as safe houses in the streets, a useful stepping-stone before moving the children on to either being off the streets or going back to their parents. Shelters are often set up by very well-intentioned citizens wanting to address the problem of street children. The most immediate way that they can do this is by providing a shelter open to the children, where they can come to get away from the streets. Although many of these shelters do sterling work, I believe the real solution to the problem will not exist in a project where street children remain street children by day and have a roof overhead at night. The trouble is lack of finances, leaving people saying that the only available provision is a shelter or nothing, or that at least a shelter must be provided first, 'then let's see what we can progress to'. The problem with the shelter scenario is that often the children never break from the trappings of street life, including glue-sniffing, prostitution and begging. Some shelters have educational facilities attached to them but the success rate is very low due to the sporadic and erratic attendance of the children who, on the one hand, have the opportunity to study and on the other hand have all the daily temptations of the streets.

Obviously, the ideal would be to return street children to their own functioning families but of course this is not always possible especially because if there were no problems at home they probably would not be in the streets in the first place. So there remains a desperate need for full-time, residential, childcare facilities. One of the most important factors for the residential projects is for them to be within a community area, in other words inside one of the black townships. I have seen projects situated on farms and others out of town and my opinion is that although the children often grow up with a lot of space, peace and quiet, the one thing that they do miss out on is community involvement. They become very inward-looking, relying on themselves for all their social needs, and start to feel cut off from mainstream society. The ideal would possibly be to have large grounds on the outskirts of a community area to get the best of both worlds; of course, this is not always possible. Whatever happens, the children need to grow up as part of the community. Otherwise when they reach eighteen or twenty-one it will be particularly difficult for them to re-enter their own society.

Children's homes

Some shelters progress to qualifying as a 'place of safety' which works on the same basis as a shelter but may have better facilities, as achieving this status gives eligibility for a government grant. The term 'place of safety' is the government term which enables the project to have children placed officially with them by government social workers or by the children's courts. 'Places of safety' receive a fairly minimal government subsidy per child and would also benefit from the help of government social workers, however, not on a full-time basis.

It is only when a project qualifies to become a children's home that government funding increases to a slightly more realistic level and the project also becomes eligible for one or more full-time, government-funded social workers, depending on how many children are at the project. Children's homes are often the most pleasant places for children to live simply due to the fact that there are more funds available to employ staff and improve facilities. However, the catch-22 situation is that to achieve status as a children's home the project has to have reached the standards of a white children's home so, in effect, the government will support a project that is already supported but is reluctant to help struggling projects.

At the end of the day the only people who can really set up projects are those with private backing. This means that projects are usually started by white, middle-class, business people who may have compassion for the kids but are culturally insensitive and try simply to imitate white children's homes. This can be damaging to the children and to their sense of culture, and the community feels isolated from such projects when they are situated right under their noses. These projects have mostly white trustees or strategically placed friendly black faces and often live in fear of 'black hijack', in other words, a black perspective. In the new South Africa, a board of directors of a children's project has to be proportionally representative of the children that they deal with, so often the race is on to find black faces that will still say, 'yes, baas'. It is not unusual for projects in South Africa to have black ground staff, even black lower management, but predominantly white decision-makers. Such projects thus remain supposedly 'safe'.

The running of a good street children project starts at the top, in as much as you need a good, committed board of trustees willing to be creative and to support the ground-level managers. These people should be a support and encouragement for the rest of the project and must consist of people committed to the welfare of children. Hidden political or financial agendas and egotistical personalities can often cause major problems when projects start to become successful, so one needs to be very careful when setting up a board of directors.

It is not really that nobody cares about the plight of street children in South Africa. I have met many concerned individuals from all communities in South Africa during my time in the country. Due to the terrifyingly huge extent of the problems it does, however, require pristine management and creative tactics to be able to draw in these people, offering a way for them to get involved. People literally do not know how to become involved in helping street children; whether they should give the children money or if this is not the best idea for them; or whether they should feed the children regularly or if this is not safe for them. Finding a way for concerned citizens to become actively involved may prove to be a real asset for projects. It is these people who may be able to change the attitudes of the general public towards street children.

I mentioned that there are no specific guidelines designed for outreach to street children yet to be successful the decision-makers must be completely in touch with the children and able to understand the struggles they face as individuals. It is not just a case of putting 'houseparents' into place and saying to the street kids, 'Right we're open.' There are so many areas to consider. Traumatised street kids need special consideration due to their horrific pasts of abuse and neglect, and to the horrendous acts of physical and sexual violence that they have so often witnessed or been victims of. Sufficient counselling mechanisms are vital to encourage them as human beings and to affirm their personalities, drawing out and focusing on their strengths and resources. A residential care project for street children needs to be so much more than a house with houseparents. In a sense, it needs to be a sanctuary where they go to receive healing for the wounds of their pasts. This is an aspect that is not often taken into account.

It is unfortunate that the social work profession does not train its workers in how to actively be part of the specific healing process of street children. While the profession may be strong in other areas, it has not taken on its responsibility to street children in a ground-level way by incorporating street children work into their training. It may not necessarily be the fault of those teaching and deciding the curriculum for social work training because there are no recognised guidelines, no books on the matter and very few tried and tested roads to street children rehabilitation. Successful projects often remain in isolation. Because there are no real avenues for their recognition, their successes in the lives of individuals often remain unknown, and where they could encourage other projects anonymity remains.

Perhaps what is needed is a paper with suggestions of methods to use when serving a street child which have been successful elsewhere. Street children so often remain guinea-pigs in the projects because the concept of taking on our responsibility to the street children is such a new one, and there is no real national forum.

Never has there been a time as urgent as now to sort out the whole area of street children in South Africa and to set up a creative structure to attempt to deal with the problem. The reason for this is the AIDS time bomb that I explained in Chapter 4. Without wishing to preach doom and gloom, South Africa will explode with AIDS and street children will just die unnoticed if we do not do something. Of course, it is of national importance to tackle the issue from within the communities and I realise that whatever we try and do for the street children, many of whom may be AIDS orphans, will still only be crisis management, an emergency plan. Who is going to save the street children? Will they die anonymously in poverty or will South Africa be able to pull itself together collectively to deal with the greater issues surrounding street kids before the inevitable onslaught of AIDS? Of course AIDS is already here; the bomb has arrived, it is ticking away and ready to explode. When it does, will we be ready?

As we can see, a centralised collective strategy is vital at this stage and one way that the projects can contribute to this is by changing the existing culture of professional jealousy between the various different projects that I have seen in most of the major cities. Many of the projects are in competition with each other for the small amounts of government grant or local funding available, but now is the time that they need to work together and to stop protecting their little empires. Nobody can own the street children work in a particular area. Inclusivity is the only way to move forward, exclusivity would lead to almost certain failure. Collective thinking and long-term networking may give birth to a long-awaited system of love, care and forward thinking.

There are two schools of thought when it comes to helping the street children and one, in my opinion, is potentially dangerous. First, there are those who from compassionate viewpoints want to help street children in a humane and rehabilitative manner; in effect, the beneficiaries are the children. However, there are also those who get involved for very different reasons. They are often businessmen or concerned citizens worried about the 'urban decay' in their city and the effect that it has on the economy and their businesses. They are predominantly concerned with violence in the area and want to get rid of the street children with the main beneficiaries then being themselves and the economy. It is important we do not naively dismiss their notion of wanting to improve business and tourism and in turn the economy, because this would help the very communities where these children come from and the country as a whole.

We need to draw this second group of thinkers in. However, any initiative born solely out of this thinking – in other words, using the 'out of sight out of mind' theory – will inevitably put the emphasis on cleaning the streets at any cost rather than developing a humane system that treats the children as the victims. There are often serious amounts of money made available by such thinkers, but the trouble is that they want specific results in line with their thinking and they want them now. When the people who are running the projects try to explain that perhaps the problem is deeper than this and may take more time and that indeed individual successes in children's lives are the real results, the donors start complaining, saying 'Why do we still see street kids on the streets when we have paid you money?' Often projects that have been given the money in this way end up having to suffer endless criticism and the picking to bits of their project. I feel sorry for the ground-level workers in these projects because they often earn very small salaries, working endless hours so selflessly. Some areas even have police funds going into projects, yet at the same time there is no training of their own police officers on how to deal with street children. Indeed the police officers need to actually be trained by experienced street children fieldworkers.

However, incorporating the help of the business sector while having the central decision-making within the humane group may be a way that solutions can start to be explored with the two trains of thought being able to workshop together and educate each other. I do indeed think that the local community has a responsibility to support street work but the primary concern needs to be the interests of the children. If projects are set up in this manner it is fairly likely that the concerns of the business sector will benefit in the long run.

While I may have some ideas due to the fact that I have worked extensively in street children care facilities, I do not hold the key to a successful project. This must be born out of communal and inclusive thinking on a national and local level, even looking internationally. It is worth looking at places like Brazil, Guatemala, Honduras and many other countries where certain organisations are much further along the road to finding solutions than we are in South Africa. Over the three and a half years that I was at Isaiah 58 we tried to take the project from a small shack in the bush for twenty children to a burgeoning, fully functioning, well-staffed childcare centre catering for 130 former street children. In that period there were many new areas that we had to look into and only through team effort were we able to address them and come out with some sort of plan.

In the early days of Isaiah 58 we had no money and no real support. Apartheid had not formally been abolished and there was no real infrastructure within the welfare department to fund projects for black children. Isaiah 58 barely survived and probably did so only due to the faith of the children and staff. In those early days there were no social workers involved and trying to get support for projects such as Isaiah 58 was very difficult because they did not meet the government's requirements. We, like many other projects, were faced with an impossible and ludicrous situation where they would not support us until they saw a concerted effort to improve the conditions of the project. In other words, they would support the organisations that already had support. How on earth were we supposed to get support in those early days? It seemed that the government did not trust the people running black, township projects and the kids were certainly not seen as important enough at that time. For the first few years we battled with the local welfare department to get some support and I remember sitting in countless meetings with a particularly helpful government social worker who guided us as to how to match up to the requirements. After landing a few large outside donations resulting in a new brick building, Isaiah 58 finally became eligible to become a 'place of safety'; not yet a children's home, which attracted a higher grant level. We again needed more outside help to build and improve before the government would register us as a children's home, although at this stage we already had more than seventy children.

However, with a combination of increased outside support for the project and more and more meetings of the welfare department it was not long until we qualified to be registered as a children's home. During the months that we had battled on to become a registered children's home we had not been entitled to funds towards employing a social worker. Being registered as a government-subsidised children's home meant an increase in subsidy levels to pay for the basic needs of the children. This in turn enabled us to use any other money we raised solely for the forwarding and developing of the project. It also meant that Isaiah 58 was eligible to employ a government-subsidised social worker.

Life in the homes

On ground level a vibrant, dedicated team is required. Houseparents and childcare workers have traditionally looked after street children projects twenty-four hours a day. I agree that they are very important but I also believe that there needs to be a greater supportive team on the ground. I have seen far too many projects that completely wear out and physically drain their houseparents. They often pay unrealistically low wages while the staff work like slaves as mothers and fathers to the children with very little time off. These houseparents end up totally burnt out, not to mention neglecting their own children living back in the townships. A supportive, vibrant team needs to include a general manager, a team specifically to cater for the recreational sports and fun needs of the children, a social work team, a fund-raiser or fund-raising team, a public relations officer, a domestic team and local as well as perhaps international volunteers to support the full-time workers. There are many other areas that need to be considered, like those of careers advice and youth skills training.

During my time at Isaiah 58, one of the jobs that I took on was to help the kids to have fun and lots of it! Every Saturday we would try to arrange a variety of excursions for all the kids, such as beach trips, zoo trips and visits to the local game reserve. I particularly enjoyed the beach trips; we would pick a heavily lifeguarded beach for maximum safety. I would try to organise local volunteers to help look after the kids and for the entire day the kids would have fun. Some of the kids even learned to surf! For those of you not familiar with surfing, surfers make it look easy. However, it takes years to learn and most people take quite some time to even stand up. Two of the Isaiah 58 boys who tried surfing for the first time, Patrick and Mzwandile, stood up on their first time out! Patrick even checked left and right, looking which way he was going to go down the line, then stood up and rode the wave. I was amazed – he was a natural.

The weather and glorious beaches in East London and Durban lend themselves to beach trips such as these, which is why they became regular events. The kids would play or swim and then spend the rest of the day getting wet, then rolling around in the sand, baking like a cake. Their behaviour was great and members of the public would often come and join in the fun, sometimes even donating money or food. We would then buy some cheap *boerwors* (South African sausage) and bread, and would have a barbecue on the beach.

Sometimes we would go to the Orient swimming pools on the beachfront in East London where the kids would play for hours on end under the careful supervision of the local lifeguards. Another favourite was loading up the pick-up truck and going off to a local game park where we would drive around searching for giraffe, zebra, bush buck and other wonderful creatures. The children looked with particular humour at the ostrich that would follow the truck, until one day it poked its head through the window and I heard a petrified scream from all the children in the back.

If the weather wasn't up to scratch and funds were available we would take the children out to the local cinema to watch movies. They loved this and I discovered a strange phenomenon about the children of South Africa – they are experts in the area of karate movies and their heroes are such people as Jackie Chan, Jet Lei, Bruce Lee, Jean Claude van Dam and Arnold Schwarzenegger. They know everything about these movie stars, every film they ever starred in, and I started to wonder how on earth they would know so much when almost all of them came from deprived areas where they wouldn't have access to video machines or televisions. What I discovered was that there was a cheap cinema in town where for the equivalent of fifty pence they could watch two movies in a row. The children would beg for the money to watch these movies. In one of the projects that I worked at I even got the nickname 'Jason' after one of the 'power rangers' because they thought I looked like him – unfortunately I did not know who they were talking about!

Of course there were plenty of fun activities that could be arranged on-site as well. We tried to explore creative avenues at the project to keep the children occupied during designated times of recreation and fun. Some of the activities that I used were football training, basketball training (once we had built a court), netball, video evenings, mini cricket, marbles, and many others. Some of the children were able to join outside activities; a few of the girls chose to go to dancing classes and got involved with drum majorettes and some of the boys joined outside soccer teams. Some of the children who were attending outside schools were able to get involved in a wealth of school activities in the afternoons.

It is very important to get the local community involved in some of the afternoon activities. My friend Patrick Lottering is a qualified sports and swimming trainer working for the Department of Sports and Recreation. He helped us launch a massive swimming programme where all of the Isaiah 58 children trained on various days. The children loved it. Pat put in a lot of hard work and time for the benefit of the kids, for many of whom it was the first time that they had swum in a pool. By the end of the course most of the children could swim. He even taught some of the older boys to paddle surf skis (a cross between surfboards and canoes), first showing them how in the pool and then taking them into the sea.

Patrick and his wife Hayley have actually become my closest friends and allies. Pat has given me a lot of political and practical advice and has really put me in touch with the community and the ANC. I am really grateful to him. He is a man dedicated to social justice and the poor, and a real friend. Hayley has also spoilt me rotten by always feeding me with huge curries, rice, chicken and many other wonderful delights. To them I am very thankful.

An exciting and loving social work team must be an integral part of the project as most of the children who will arrive at the project will have significant emotional baggage that needs lots of love, counselling and encouragement. The social work team will be able to apply itself to the problems and the needs of the children as this is an area that houseparents are not trained to deal with and indeed it is too much for them to try and take on. I'm not a social worker and therefore not an expert to speak on internal social work structures. But I suspect there is a need to look at new ideas, perhaps to take proven ways of counselling children and adapting them to cater for street children. They will be able to talk with the children on a one-to-one basis and to start activities like group therapy, encouraging the children to open up and to work through some of the trauma of their lives.

So far we have the housemothers and housefathers whose role is to be the parental part of the project, the fun recreational team to keep the children occupied and entertained, and the social work team. It is also very important to have a team of domestic workers, primarily because in these projects it so often becomes another job for the houseparents to do all the cleaning and cooking for the children. Obviously a domestic team would be solely dedicated to doing this, but it is important that the children are taught some responsibilities as well so it may be an idea for the houseparents to assign children to help the domestic team on different days.

One way of adding extra person-power to the project without extra expense is to utilise local and foreign volunteers. Volunteers are usually really keen to get involved, to get their hands dirty and to simply serve the organisation. They can be a real asset and take the pressure off the full-time staff as they are valuable workers and, what's more, they are free.

The one aspect of residential projects that I have not touched on is that of education. In each of the organisations that I've worked in I have focused on the child development side in collaboration with somebody else or other organisations looking after the purely educational side of the development. At Isaiah 58 there was a wonderful bridging school run by a local teacher, originally from Canada who was fluent in Xhosa, called Gaye Oosthuizen. The idea was simple. As the street children had missed out on so much education while being on the streets, it was often very difficult for them to be integrated straight back into education because they would have to go into a lower standard with children much younger than themselves. This would be very depressing for them and would do nothing to improve their self-esteem. What the bridging schools were able to do was to give specialised education with a pupil–teacher ratio that allowed each child more personal input from the teacher. The children were able to progress at their own pace and some children could achieve more than one standard in a year. In fact one boy named Patrick (the same boy that did so well surfing) was able to achieve three standards in one year through working really hard. Those children who did not need bridging school were filtered straight through into the local township schools and, of course, we at Isaiah 58 closely monitored their development at the schools, as would any parental body.

Nothing quite prepared me emotionally for my first Father's Day at the project. It is one of my fondest memories. I hadn't really thought about the possible implications that Father's Day might bring for me at Isaiah 58. When the children returned from school on that particular day I was bombarded by one hundred hugs and Father's Day cards with drawings. I could not believe it. We were very short staffed and I was the only male worker at the time. It was a deeply moving experience for which I am grateful to God. This happened every Father's Day that I was at Isaiah 58.

In later years I was even invited to take part in the Father's Day activities at one of the local schools in the township. It was a hilarious day. All the fathers of the schoolchildren were invited to an assembly for a special thanksgiving service for which about fifty were present. When I walked in as one of the fathers, the other fathers couldn't stop staring at me as I was the only white person there out of all the parents, teachers and children. I could just imagine them thinking, 'Who is his child and what is his story?'

I sat there conspicuously with all the other fathers. After the service the principal said to the children, 'Now, if your father is here, go and give him his present.' The present was a drawing. At once there was a stampede of about thirty children all running towards me to give me a gift. I wish I'd had a video camera that day to capture the look on everyone's face. I even got kids I didn't know running to me!

To enable your ground-level team to function properly it is very important for the project to have a good fund-raiser or fund-raising team that can canvass for support locally, nationally and internationally because to set up a proper team and to be able to cater for the needs of many children you need plenty of financial backing. A public relations officer is also a good idea as the project must be and must be seen to be actively involved in and an integral part of the local community. It is important for the project to have a high profile in the city or town that it serves. The fund-raising team and the public relations officer would probably work very closely together from the administration offices.

The Isaiah 58 pick-up truck with myself and Auntie Maggie at the helm with many children in the back became a familiar sight around Duncan Village, Buffalo Flats and most areas of East London and we had a lot of fun together. I went to a number of community occasions with Auntie Maggie and the children and among these were many funerals. Funerals are a big thing in Xhosa society and it is very important to attend funerals of people that you know as it is a real sign of respect for the family. The services are fairly long, after which there is a traditional motorcade of vehicles with their headlights on; this pro-ceeds at a snail's pace, completely snarling up every road in the township to the graveyard where everybody parks and goes to the burial site. This is then followed by a great feast, sometimes cows and pigs are slaughtered. It is traditionally important to make the funeral as huge as possible with lots of food and speeches.

Auntie Maggie and myself and about twenty children had just attended the funeral of a member of the community, and getting out of the area of the church was proving to be very difficult because of the crowds, so I took a back route and rejoined the motorcade on its way to the burial site. When we got to the graveyard we parked and got out of the vehicle and walked quietly over to the grave side where the crowd had gathered and the coffin was waiting to be lowered. As we waited in silence, solemnly, I started looking around and realised that I did not recognise anyone in the crowds and also that everybody was staring at us. A few moments later a man wandered over to me and whispered very gently into my ear, saying, 'I think you want that funeral over there', pointing to the other side of the grave-yard where the crowd from our funeral had gathered. In my rush to escape the crowds at the church I had joined the wrong motorcade and marched twenty kids straight into the wrong funeral. It was so embarrassing as we walked away and rejoined the other funeral. Auntie Maggie still laughs about that day.

Isaiah 58 was exciting, front-line living and I remember walking through the grounds on many occasions thanking God and saying that there was no other job in the world that I would rather be doing. For a period of time I was completely and totally satisfied and at peace, knowing my calling and absolutely loving the job that God had called me to. There were many fun events during this time and one of the highlights for me was Christmas-time each year. It was fantastic. The most exciting would naturally be the first one that we shared together and that one set the precedent for those that followed. I had been aware that the children had never celebrated Christmas before. Christmas celebrations are often so Westernised so, not surprisingly, Christmas has much less traditional meaning in Xhosa but Xhosa Christians do still celebrate it, but with much less buying and present-giving, yet with much merriment, eating and huge celebratory church services.

I did not want to force my Western culture on to the children by celebrating Christmas my way but I wanted to show the kids that indeed we thought they were special and wanted to celebrate the symbol of Christ's birth with them in a fun way. With the help of a donation from some UK supporters, I was able to put on a programme of Christmas fun for the children. In South Africa December is the summer holidays, similar to those of July and August in the UK, and Christmas becomes a time when we have a real job on our hands to keep the kids occupied. In the first December we spent many days having fun on the beach as well as having video days and fun days back at camp.

I wanted to give the kids a holiday that would blow their proverbial socks off so Auntie Maggie and I got busy buying a 'small' present for each child as a gift at Christmas. We then bought a tree. Strictly speaking the word 'tree' is a slight exaggeration and 'branch of tree size' would probably be a slightly better description. This hilarious-looking thing was decorated by the kids and put on the end of the shack along with decorations lining the walls. This was a good creative exercise for the kids to get involved in and they really enjoyed it.

Next, Auntie and I went to buy the food. Now, Auntie Maggie knows food; she is guaranteed to put two stone on anyone who stays with her for more than fifteen minutes. She loves food – preparing it and eating it. She was determined to make this Christmas meal epic, and epic it was. We had about six different meats, and an array of vegetables fit for Mandela himself. The children all pulled crackers, wore party hats, sang songs, played games and obviously ate lots and lots of food. It was a feast, a celebration, a family Christmas. When I was a child, Christmas had a sense of magic and I wanted to give a little bit of the magic to the children. The children did not know that we had bought them presents and at midnight I crept around the project putting presents on individual beds. Auntie Maggie thought I was mad but enjoyed the fun any way. Once one kid realised that there was a present at the end of their bed the rest of the kids awoke like a Mexican wave.

It was brilliant, pure happiness; the kids had never experienced anything like it; it was a wonderful moment. The children had not really had an opportunity like this to just relax and enjoy the fun. They could not quite believe how many parties and fun events that happened during that time. It just meant that each year we had to live up to the year before. The celebrations lasted until the New Year when of course we stayed up until midnight to see in 1994.

Auntie Maggie and I played an array of different roles with the children and it wasn't long before we became very familiar with the inside of the accident unit at the local hospital, whether it was racing stabbed street children to the emergency unit after being attacked or taking injured children from Isaiah 58 after playing. With 120 children living at Isaiah 58 I was bound to visit there once in a while.

On one occasion Vukani, one of the Isaiah 58 boys, was playing cricket in the mud cricket area that we had at the project. As he slid in to make a run, he must have caught a piece of rock in the ground and he cut what just looked like a huge piece of steak approximately six inches long and four inches wide out of his calf. I've never seen a flap of skin and meat so huge; it literally went down to the bone. At first it did not bleed that much, surprisingly, and I picked him up and raced him down to the local hospital. As we got going, the blood soon started to pour out. Vukani had to stay in hospital for two weeks and had skin grafts to help heal the wounds. One thing I learnt at Isaiah 58 was that anything can happen any time.

Another incident occurred when Ncediswa was walking home from school and stepped off the pavement into the path of a fast, oncoming car. She was really knocked for six and sustained quite massive head injuries, a gruesome degloving to one of her hands and various cuts and bruises all over the body. Because the injuries looked so horrific everybody in the area just froze, and suddenly I felt the responsibility fall on to my shoulders. I ran towards the child who was unconscious, but I realised that she was still alive. As I was running I called for an ambulance on the mobile phone; we then waited, and waited and waited. Soon she came to and I attempted to comfort her but it wasn't long before she was screaming and kicking. She was in real pain and it became obvious she had no neck injuries or back injuries so we deemed it safe enough to get to hospital ourselves. I will always remember that day because one of the community members called Mark was there with his little sports-style car. We put Ncediswa inside and rushed her off to the hospital. For some reason that I will never know he had a siren in his car which he promptly switched on as we raced like VIPs to the emergency rooms! Although the girl looked in a bad way and stayed in hospital for some weeks, miraculously she had no lasting damage. God had really had his hand on her.

A slightly different memory of the local hospital was the occasion when I took one of the boys named Mzwandile in for an operation to have his extremely squint eyes straightened. It had always been extremely noticeable that his eyes did not work or move properly; he had one of the worst squints that I had ever seen. It worried me so much that I took him off to see a specialist and after a consultation I decided to take him for an operation. After having this operation he had perfectly straight eyes which was not only a physical boost for him but also a psychological encouragement. The operation had not gone quite without incident as, when he was taken down to theatre for the operation, he took one look at the equipment, jumped off the emergency table and tried to run away! One of the doctors had to sprint after him and retrieve him.

There are so many stories from the days of Isaiah 58 that I could go on endlessly! My time there was one of the happiest episodes of my life and I still dearly love those children and keep in contact with them. Sometimes they phone me to say how things are going, and at other times when I visit East London I call by and see them. They will always have a special place in my heart. I miss laughing and chatting to Auntie Maggie while eating *mvubo*, a mixture of African salad (mielie-meal, a corn-based traditional African dish) and *amasi* (sour milk). We did have a lot of fun and were able to work together as a team. Auntie Maggie had an amazing gift of being able to forgive and forget after arguments. It is not that we had that many arguments but after she had disciplined one of the children, once that child had apologised, she always welcomed them back into her loving arms, just like a mother should, never holding a grudge. She worked very hard for the children, living on site and never taking any holiday; they were her family. I was very fortunate to be able to work alongside Auntie Maggie and I am very grateful to her.

I mentioned at the beginning of this chapter that there seemed to be a spiritual presence at Isaiah 58 and indeed spiritual understanding among the children. It was therefore ironic and perhaps symbolic that the day of Siseko Sisulu's death was the same day that all the older Isaiah 58 boys were baptised in the church that they were attending. They had not been forced to do this. It was a commitment based on free will and was indeed a great moment to see many of these boys that I had known on the streets deciding to make a serious commitment to following Christ. We had a service where some of the boys played in the church band and then went to a local swimming pool where the boys were baptised in front of the church members. I stood there with tears in my eyes. I also feel that it was symbolic as obviously sinister forces were at play in the death of Siseko and it was as if God struck back, reclaiming his children in a dynamic way. For me personally it symbolised that although evil had been responsible for taking Siseko, love could win and now even Siseko was with the Lord.

At the end of 1996 I resigned from Isaiah 58. The project was now well established and well supported and had a strong local staff who could continue the work. Isaiah 58 was also full by this stage and I was still committed to working on the streets and getting the children out of street life. I decided to take up an offer from another East London street children project called the Daily Bread Charitable Trust. I visited England to sort out my work permits and for a time of spiritual, mental and physical renewal as well as to complete what was to be a successful fund-raising tour for my future work with street children.

6 Steps in the right direction

During my time in South Africa I have seen many miracles – some of them on the streets, some in the children's homes – and I feel that I've been very fortunate to witness so many street children overcoming their situation through the power of God and the strengths of communities. Many of these children's backgrounds are the same and the abuses similar, yet each child is so individually special. This chapter is dedicated purely to telling some of the stories of hope. There appear to be so many children with individual personal successes in their lives but I picked a few typical scenarios and one or two slightly different stories.

The first story is of a girl who I first met in 1993. Her nickname at the time was 'Nombitshi', and this translated means 'ugly'. I had first met her on the streets of East London and she instantly touched my heart. She was eleven at the time and used to live with her older sister and the other older girls who were caught up in child prostitution. These girls were part of a larger group of boys and girls who were heavily involved with sniffing benzine. I remember her on the street; she would be wearing about three layers of clothes and a 'beanie' hat. She was filthy and used to trail behind her sister. The group used to live under the skateboard ramp that had been built for the white children in the area. They had grown tired of it and it was left unused. There was a room under the ramp previously used for selling cool drinks. This room was now home for about twelve street children. I was deeply concerned about her as she was the youngest girl in the group at the time and a certain target for abuse. However, the attachment to her sister was all that she had. I started to pray to God for a miracle to save her as I knew that she would soon be lost to the streets.

I kept on helping her each day until one day when all of the children of Isaiah 58 went to a carol service in town. The venue was opposite the skateboard park, or so we thought. It was another one of my classic mix-ups. I had got the venues mixed up and marched the kids into a very professional choral concert. Confused, we left again as the kids were bored, and waited outside. I went over to talk to the local street children and after a while they came and started talking to Auntie Maggie and the Isaiah 58 children. This was great because it showed Nombitshi that there were people that she knew at Isaiah 58. It made the thought of living there less daunting.

I asked her if she would like to go to the project and she said 'yes' but then looked at her sister and quickly added, 'tomorrow'. The next day she was ready and waiting. She later told me that she could not believe that I had come back for her. She settled at Isaiah 58 for a while but she was very difficult and hard to handle; she was extremely rebellious. She ran away three times and each time the Lord miraculously led me to where she was in the township or on the streets.

After the third time of running away I was chatting with her and I suddenly thought about the implications of having a name like 'ugly'. What must this be doing to her self-esteem? What did it communicate to her about who she was as a person? I did not know much Xhosa at the time but I did know that most female names were preceded with the letters 'no'. I found out the word for 'beautiful' in Xhosa which was *mhle*, and added the other letters to it making the word 'Nomhle'. I checked with a few Xhosa friends who told me that this was indeed a Xhosa name.

I called the girl over and told her that I was going to rename her Nomhle and would call her that from now on.

Her face lit up and her self-love increased from that moment on, so much so that from that day on she settled without running away ever again. She could hardly stop smiling as she walked out to write her new name on all her schoolbooks.

As we see from Nomhle's story, street work – actually going out to and becoming part of the streets – is the key to building up relationships with the street children. Many of my evenings are spent on the streets in the company of the street kids, today in Durban and formerly in East London.

Of the miracles that I have seen, one of the most heartening is how the number of street children in East London has decreased over the last six years, so much so that there are only a handful of kids left on the streets there. In the early days there were many children in the streets and they were usually very dependent on the sniffing of benzine. However, through constant street work and organisations to house the children, the numbers of street children have been greatly reduced. There are always new children coming on to the streets but because there are not so many kids actually in the streets it is less of a temptation for township children to stay on the streets. One of the other interesting facts is that we have got rid of almost all of the benzine sniffing within the under-eighteen age group. Indeed the only people sniffing benzine now are the former street children over the age of eighteen still living on the streets.

There have been other elements to bring into consideration when analysing the drop in number of street children. One of those is the fact that many of the street children who have not come through to the projects have been arrested for petty crime and occasionally serious crime. There are many former street children sitting in East London Prison at the moment, the youngest have now been sent or are waiting to be sent to reform school away from the area and the older ones have long prison sentences.

Today East London's streets are very different to those of

six years ago. When I'm in East London I drive around the old haunts, checking if there are any street children about. The old street corners that used to be so familiar to street children are often empty now. The area of Southernwood that used to be the worst area for street children no longer seems to be an attractive place for the children. The only people left living street life there are the children of three, four, five years ago like Felicia, Nomsa and their boyfriends. These girls are now eighteen years old and their boyfriends are even older. In fact, there is only one child living in that group now. Her name is Thandi and she is fourteen years old. Sadly, I have been trying to serve Thandi for about four years, having taken her into both Isaiah 58 and Daily Bread but she does not seem able to make the transition. She breaks my heart.

The Quigney area of East London including the beachfront still has a handful of young boys who don't actually live in the street but are staying in shacks in the bushes down by the beach. They are not sniffing glue or benzine and are not involved in child prostitution but are quite heavily involved in car- and house-breaking and smoking marijuana as they are living with older bush dwellers. They are well dressed and do not want to go to any of the projects as they are not really suffering the hardships of street life, are making money and have their freedom. I do not think this group will last long because one by one they will be arrested as time goes on and fortunately no new children seem to be joining the group. I do visit these boys when I am in East London and I get on very well with them. I have known some since they were very small and they trust me; indeed some of them have stayed at the projects I've been involved in at one time or another.

It seems that the whole dynamic of the street children has changed in East London. The trend of children running to the streets seems to have stopped. I do not mean to say that it will never be a problem again but for the time being we have achieved many of our goals and it is up to the residential care facilities to continue their good work in rehabilitating the street children of the last six years. It is also worth mentioning that it is a very opportune time for the projects of East London to start preparing for the onslaught of AIDS.

As I said before, street work seems to be the key to working with street children. What I found to be most effective in East London, and what I do now in Durban to make initial relationships with the kids is to simply sit and chat or play games with the children, sometimes eating food with them and always being ready to listen to their problems. This in turn leads to being able to help them in practical ways. When you know the street children well, they start introducing you to new arrivals as soon as they arrive on the streets. One particular night in East London, I was talking to a familiar group of street children in the beachfront area when they introduced me to three new boys who had arrived that day from King Williams Town. Two of them had come from further afield, their names were Zwolakhe and Sipho. Zwolakhe was a young boy aged ten who fled his home after becoming a victim of physical abuse. He had been repeatedly burned on a stove and beaten up by family members. He had then escaped to an uncle who also physically abused him. It was then that he decided to run to the streets and on arrival he met up with a streetwise boy called Michael about whom little is known. Zwolakhe and Michael met up with a third lad, a 13-year-old boy called Sipho who was well educated, fluent in English and from a well-to-do background. He had even been to school at the prestigious Robin Hood College in Johannesburg but due to problems at home had run away to his grandparents in the Transkei and from there on to the streets.

These boys had moved around from Queenstown to King Williams Town to East London and had finally ended up on the beachfront with the group of kids that I was very familiar with. God put them right into contact with me at a stage that was vital to their future. Their arrival into a crowd of children involved in sniffing benzine and prostitution put them at risk. Up to this stage they had not really been part of the harsh realities of street life because Queenstown and King Williams Town are much smaller places and street life is not quite so dangerous there.

I told them about Isaiah 58. The boys were obviously frightened on the streets so they jumped at the chance to visit the Isaiah 58 project. It was late at night and it would have been unfair on the housemothers at Isaiah 58 if I had descended on the place at that time so I decided to take them the next morning. I told the boys that I would meet them first thing in the morning outside the 'Spur', a local family restaurant, where we happened to be standing at that moment. The boys seemed eager and I will never forget the next morning when I arrived to pick them up. Sipho had slept on the pavement outside the restaurant to ensure that there was no way that I would miss them. He looked relieved when I approached him and when I asked him where the others were he pointed towards the bushes by the swimming pools. As I approached them I noticed Zwolakhe tucked into a bush holding his T-shirt stretched over his head. He was actually sleeping curled up in a small wooden crate used for packaging oranges! Michael approached a little later but I believe that he had a home to go to because he didn't seem desperate to get off the streets. However, I took all three of them to Isaiah 58 for assessment and after a few days, as I suspected, Michael had absconded and we heard that he was back in King Williams Town. Zwolakhe and Sipho stayed on at Isaiah 58 where they lived in peace and attempted to put the pieces of their lives back together.

Zwolakhe still lives at Isaiah 58. He is a happy 13-year-old boy with a great sense of humour, a raspy voice and a bright laugh. He is progressing well at school and is very happy enjoying his childhood. Sipho is now sixteen years old, about to turn seventeen, and has left Isaiah 58 and now lives at the Daily Bread project in East London. I still keep in contact with him especially as he has shown a real interest in working with street children himself in the future. He is a brilliant child and I would love so much to be able to work with him one day. He has been back to Johannesburg to visit his parents and his uncle in Soweto but feels happier living in East London. He also attends one of the local churches regularly and since being baptised at Isaiah 58 has continued his commitment to God.

The 'street group' that Sipho and Zwolakhe had become involved in was a particular group that was instantly hazardous for youngsters who join it. It is this very group that Sinovuyo had grown out of and that Siseko had joined before being killed. Two other boys who instantly joined that group on arrival to the streets were Luvuyo and Velile. Luvuyo had originally run away from a difficult family situation in Queenstown and had arrived in East London where some other children had been shown the East London rubbish dump, a place where a whole community scavenges for survival amid the refuse. At first he was excited by the sweets that used to be dumped from the local sweet factory and easily made friends with the other rubbish dump kids, one in particular called Velile. Luvuyo moved into a shack belonging to Velile's mother but after a while life on the rubbish dumps didn't seem quite so exciting and the reality of extreme poverty and violence set in. It was a particularly bad time for gang violence, and many people were being shot and houses were being burned regularly. The two boys decided to go to town together in search of a better life. They were attracted by the clean city streets and the opportunity to beg. When they arrived, however, they met up with the 'Southernwood' crowd who immediately welcomed them into the group. Felicia and Nomsa genuinely liked their company but it was not healthy for the boys as both of these girls were completely caught up in a life of benzine abuse and prostitution. The two boys themselves instantly became benzine sniffers and each time I used to see them they would be wasted, hardly able to stand up. However, life was not yet unbearable for them. I remember Luvuyo used to stand dwarfed in a long, thick, trench coat many sizes too big for him and the boys soon became typical street children, dressed in rags, dirty and constantly high.

One night the two boys were attacked by a group of other street dwellers, and stabbed in the back. It was miraculous that both stabbings missed all major organs, but they both have distinct scars now on their upper backs. They both ended up at the hospital that night – it was a great shock to both of them and suddenly they realised that yet again they were suffering. I had kept in contact with them daily throughout their time on the streets, always encouraging them to leave the streets. After the stabbing they finally felt that they were ready to go. Instantly I seized the opportunity and brought them to the Isaiah 58 project. The boys settled well; God had been watching over them. This was made particularly evident as within a few months of taking the boys in, Velile's mother passed away from an illness which meant they would not have had anywhere to go back to, even if they had wished to return.

Both of these boys stayed happily at Isaiah 58 for two years before moving on to the Daily Bread project in 1997 where they now both stay. Luvuyo has made a visit back to Queenstown to be reunited with his parents for the first time in three years which was very successful although he will continue to live in the children's home at which he now resides.

Luvuyo and Velile were very lucky. Sometimes people don't survive stabbing or the other trappings of street life. They were no different to Siseko; in fact they were simply the next two boys to enter the group after Siseko.

One of the first street children that I ever took off the

streets was a boy of eleven years old called Blessing who I found in the streets together with an older boy called Thandisizwe. What I didn't realise was that both boys were wanted for rape in the Transkei even though Blessing had been only ten at the time. They had fled the Transkei streets to East London where they were living in the bushes on the beachfront. Blessing may have been present during the rape but could not possibly have been the main rapist. Blessing has a peaceful disposition, almost as if he has seen too much and is trying desperately to find peace. He loves activities where people laugh and appreciate each other and found it very difficult to cope with violence.

I brought both boys into the project at the same time and it was not long before they started to find friends of their own age group. Thandisizwe was a most likeable 16-year-old boy who had a really endearing personality but was also capable of displaying a dangerous tough streak. He had the scars to show it as well, but he never did tell me where the scars came from.

After about a year he left the project and I did not see him for about two years. He has been in and out of prison for house-breaking recently. However, little Blessing, who is now fifteen years old, still resides at Isaiah 58 and remains one of the softest, most polite and most caring children ever to come through the gates. All he needed was to be loved to find his peace.

One of the things I find most amazing about my time in South Africa is how God puts me into contact with street children at the strangest of times and often when I am least expecting it. It makes me laugh because although street work puts you in contact with the children of the streets and enables you to take many children off the streets, there are many times when street work crosses over into your personal time. In fact, you soon learn that working with street children can often be a 24-hour job and God often catches you napping!

Food seems to be the proverbial carrot that God dangles in front of me while leading me to the children at risk. In 1996 I had convinced myself that a slap-up breakfast once a week at the Holiday Inn just down the road from my flat in East London would be the perfect time to think and plan the next seven days. I used to wake up at six o'clock and go down to the hotel and pile my plate with bacon, eggs, toast, sausage, tomatoes, beans and just about everything else you could imagine. The beauty of it was that it was an 'all you can eat' menu – in other words, endless! Once I was as full as could be I would sit and drink my orange juice and coffee over an hour of planning. Of course it would have been just as easy to sit at home with my Coco Pops and do the same thing for much less but I was blinded to this notion.

I got to know the kitchen staff at the hotel quite well and they used to like me because I would always chat to them in Xhosa. Once they found out that I worked with street children they were thrilled and sometimes they would chat to me for ages. One lady working there called Sunshine had four children of her own. She also had a sister who had run away, leaving another three children for her to look after. She tried very hard to look after all of the children but the problem was that she was also a single parent and did not earn enough to feed her own kids properly, let alone her sister's children. She told me that the eldest son of her sister's was trying to earn extra money in the streets of Mdantsane at the notorious street children hangout called 'highway'. This was the main taxi rank of the area and also a very dangerous, crowded area and he was fast becoming a child of the streets.

I was able to step in and find places for the sister's children at Isaiah 58. Sunshine was thrilled and visited the children often. The children themselves were also thrilled with proper food now and having a place to live. God had turned an everyday situation into the rescuing of children in need. Phaphama is now seventeen years old, loves basketball and rap music and is doing well at school. God knew that the streets would have destroyed him. Together with his younger brother and sister he lives happily at Isaiah 58.

On another occasion I was being led by my stomach again, this time to a place I knew where you could create a 'killer pizza' which for me consisted of lots of avocado, calamari (squid), a little bit of cheese – not too much – and lots of mushroom on a crispy base – superb, heaven! As I pulled up in the car, my mouth was already watering at the thought of this giant pizza about to be demolished solely by yours truly. I noticed a young boy in tatters sitting on the rubbish bin directly outside the shop, hoping to catch a kind patron for loose change or a slice of pizza. I gave my usual greeting saying, '*Sharp brah, kunjani namhlanje*' which roughly translated into English is, 'Hi, brother, how are you today!' As always, the sight of a white man suddenly greeting him in street slang brought a beaming smile to his face and we started chatting. He came from one of the squatter camps near town and was on the streets because he was living with his grandmother in poverty and she could not really look after him.

I ordered my pizza and sheepishly gave him a large slice as we continued talking. After about ten minutes and with full stomachs we were on our way to meet Auntie Maggie and the Isaiah 58 children. Bongani lived at Isaiah for three years from the age of thirteen to sixteen and now stays back in his original township area. Through a strange meeting like this one, Isaiah 58 was able to bridge the gap in Bongani's life.

It was not just food that God used to cross my path with his children. Sometimes he would catch me at moments when I was simply tired or on my way to go surfing, knowing full well that I would not turn my back on them. I remember one time walking out of the front door of my flat when I lived on the beachfront in East London. It was early in the morning, I was bleary-eyed and still trying to wake up. I'd had a late night, probably working on the streets, and didn't really feel like striking up a conversation with anyone. As I approached the gates I noticed a young boy walking past without looking up and immediately, looking at his clothing, I identified him as being a street child although I did not recognise him. Part of me wanted to let him carry on walking. I was late and needed to get to Isaiah 58. As I was stumbling to find my car keys I'm sure the Holy Spirit gave me a kick in the backside because I felt compelled to ask the boy where he was coming from, to which he replied, 'Down there by the beach.'

I said to him 'Do you live there?' to which he replied that he did. He told me that he had been in and out of another shelter in town and was back on the streets now. He did not enjoy the streets but did not want to go back to the other shelter for some reason. As I chatted with him further I could see that he was on the verge of being sucked back into street life. I told him about the Isaiah 58 project which he sounded excited about and agreed to come to visit.

The boy's name was Aviwe and he still had a lot of street life in him. One particular incident which highlighted this happened during a visit from the Amos Trust projects co-ordinator Beki Bateson. Beki was making the *Based on Hope* fund-raising video for the Trust and on one of her visits to Isaiah 58 she had left her purse in her bag in one of the rooms at the project. Later that day we realised that the wallet was gone with all her money, so were three new boys that I had brought to the project that day. When Aviwe had come to visit Isaiah 58 with me he had brought two other boys who were living down in the bushes with him. According to the other children at Isaiah 58, the other two boys had run away a couple of hours earlier and Aviwe had vanished later, presumably to join them on the streets. Now this is not the first time and certainly won't be the last time the children get themselves into trouble for theft. Beki lost a considerable amount of money that day, the temptation had just been too great for the children. However, one thing that Beki realised was that the greater problem was not her wallet and the money but the fact that Aviwe in this case felt that he could not return to the project because he was linked to the other two boys who stole the wallet. In his mind we would be furious with him and out for his blood. This unfortunate misconception made it vital to find the child as soon as possible. Although we needed to show him that theft was wrong and that he would be punished, we would also show him that he was still loved and welcome at Isaiah 58.

I got into the car and prayed simply, 'Lord, please help me find him and the wallet.' I drove from Isaiah 58 to the centre of town down one of the busy town roads called Fleet Street which runs towards the beach. Yet again God's amazing timing came into play. In a crowded town like East London it is fairly unlikely that I would know which road he had taken and even more unlikely that I should spot the child on any given road. However, as I drove down the streets I saw him striding furiously towards the beach in his little green shorts and black jersey. When he saw me he simply stopped, looking very guilty. I said to him softly, '*Khwela*' which means 'Come on, get in'. He did so and as we drove back I gave him a gentle telling off for making me so worried and told him that the stealing was wrong but his life was much, much more important.

We never did find the wallet because the two other boys had taken it and were nowhere to be found. Had Aviwe gone back to live on the streets he may not have even found those other two boys and may have had to survive on his own, putting him in great danger. Aviwe never ran away again.

Prior to being on the streets Aviwe had been living with his grandmother. He had no parents. It was his friends who encouraged him into the streets and his grandmother had not been strong enough to stop him. Street life had engulfed him; he had been abused, allegedly by white men, in a house in the Quigney area of East London where he had sought refuge. It was as if street life was a wave taking him, a wave that he was not strong enough to fight against.

He started to love Isaiah 58 and settled in very smoothly. I made the necessary arrangements with the other shelter that he had been residing in who told me that they were just glad that he was safe. Very quickly he was enrolled at one of the local schools where he began catching up on his education. After about two years he expressed an interest in being reunited with his grandmother. The 'streets' in him was long since gone and it was felt that he should return to his grandmother who was, after all, his family and capable of looking after him. She could then apply for child benefit grant.

On a visit to East London just before Christmas 1998 I bumped into Aviwe at a carnival on the beachfront. It was the first time that I had seen him in about two years and I was thrilled to see that he was really well, had no interest in street life and had continued in his education. He was very happy – it was a great reunion. I am so glad that God gave me that kick up the backside to start talking to him early on that summer's morning, and I marvel at his timing and just love being used in his plans.

Sometimes, however, children did turn up on our doorstep at Isaiah 58. Sometimes they would come on foot or on their own and at other times concerned members of the community or even the police would come in and drop children off with us. Often those that the community or police brought to us were children who had suffered abuse within the townships and needed a safe home for a short or longer period of time. One afternoon the Child Protection Unit arrived at Isaiah 58 with a little girl, seven years old. It was a cold winter's day and she was wrapped in a blanket to keep warm. I had been out on a food donations pick-up and arrived back to see this withdrawn, tearful addition to the Isaiah 58 group.

Before I entered the room that she was in, Auntie Maggie briefed me as to why she was there. Ntomboxolo had been living in a shack settlement about fifteen minutes outside East London. She was not a street child but lived with her mother and extended family in very overcrowded conditions. Living in such conditions of poverty, unemployment, lack of facilities, lack of running water and sanitation all exposed her to the probability of abuse and neglect. Ntomboxolo had been raped at the tender age of seven by her uncle. In most societies the majority of child sex abuse goes unnoticed but in this case somebody had reported it and the uncle had been caught by the police. However, it would take some time to complete the trial and Ntomboxolo was brought into Isaiah 58 for personal protection. Isaiah 58 was being used as a community oasis for children often traumatised from abuse, and like every other organisation dealing with black children at that time we were underequipped but, as there was literally nowhere else for her to go, we would rely on God and try our best.

I remember the first time that I met Ntomboxolo. I noticed that she was motionless, yet her eyes were constantly weeping, she was crying. At that moment I moved a little bit closer to trying to be able to understand the profound horror of her rape. The pain was displayed through her eyes. She had obviously suffered deep trauma and with her distant, detached look I knew that she was trying to come to terms with a brutal attack on her person and soul, feeling as if someone had ripped out her dignity and thrown it away, leaving her vulnerable, exposed and in excruciating pain. What goes on in the sick mind of someone who can inflict such pain on such a little one?

Looking at her eyes, I noticed an innocent beauty. They say that the window to a person's soul is in their eyes. I believe this to be true because without exception behind every story of rape that I see, every abused child on the streets, every little child scavenging to survive on the rubbish dumps, I always see the same thing: two glistening, beautiful, brown eyes often crying out, appealing for love, recognition, security, a future and rescue. It reminds me of driving through a game park and happening upon a newborn, frightened springbok. Just before it darts, if you get a chance to look at its eyes, you will see helpless, frightened eyes yet with a remarkable beauty. When I see the children's eyes it cuts directly and deeply into my heart. What crime did they do to receive such punishment? They are born into poverty and a struggling community. They are often terrified little children just trying to make it through life.

As I was introduced to Ntomboxolo I kept my distance, knowing full well that it was another male who had inflicted so much pain upon her earlier that day. I stretched out my hand and we safely shook hands but she did not look up at all. I knew that it would be wrong of me to launch into trying to comfort her as she was very fragile. Rebuilding her dignity, self-love and trust would be a long process that only God could really completely achieve but those people around her would also play a major role. Auntie Maggie played a pivotal role as a female counsellor especially as there are certain physical practicalities to be attended to after a rape.

I realised at that stage that in fact my role was also vital as she needed a safe, positive, male influence to help her come to terms with what had happened to her. My role was to simply be affirming, respectful, supportive, fun and ready for a game to lift her spirits for a moment.

As the weeks turned to months Ntomboxolo changed drastically for the better. The oasis of Isaiah 58 had been a refuge used to put her on the slow, gentle road to healing. After a few months she was starting to play happily. She was slightly more able to mingle with the other children and she loved playing games; the child who could not bear another person to touch her was starting to open up, to be restored.

I do not want to make light of the situation of rape by saying that she was completely healed. But after six months of interaction with Auntie Maggie, myself and 120 other children she was beginning to behave like any other child, running, taking diving leaps and forcing me to catch her. She used to jump into my arms and just hug me. I could hardly believe that it was the same girl as that of a few months earlier. Her dignity was being restored.

Every couple of weeks her mother would visit and this increased in frequency until after six months, by which time the uncle was behind bars, we felt that she was ready to go with her mother and live back home permanently. Her mother was amazed at how well she had progressed and it was a gift to watch her grow in excitement every time she came through the gates to visit Ntomboxolo. I was gutted when she left, because we had become very close but I knew it was right for her to go home. I cherished those six months with Ntomboxolo and her story of hope brings me great joy. I remember her as a bright, bubbly little 7-year-old who, after six months, was always by my side. I pray that she may now have no obstacles in her way as God continues the process of healing with her and her family. She had started to regain her peace right in front of my very eyes. I knew it was miraculous and I feel very privileged to witness God's healing hand at work.

7   A new challenge

In November 1996 after completing my work with Isaiah 58 I returned to England for six months. I had not intended for it to be such a long stay but I had to wait quite some time for my new work permit. I returned to South Africa in May '97 to work alongside an organisation called the Daily Bread Charitable Trust in a project for street children based in Durban – or so I thought. God had other plans and I was asked by the people in East London to help them 'sort out' their East London project that was experiencing problems. The children appeared to be unmanageable. They were breaking into shops and stealing from the homes that they were living in. Quite a few of them were awaiting trial or imprisoned for petty theft. The trustees, knowing of my work at Isaiah 58, asked me to try and help bring the children under control.

It was a project with over two hundred former street children residing full-time. These children had been collected over about eight years and I felt that it was the perfect opportunity to address again the problem of street children in East London which at the time was escalating again. Although we had taken many children off the streets during the Isaiah 58 period, that project was full and there were still kids on the streets. Daily Bread had a much larger capacity so I was excited by the potential of working there.

Before I started my work full-time in this new venture I went up to a little place in South Africa on the border of the Orange Free State and the Eastern Cape called Aliwal North, to visit a small residential project for street children there called Miracle House. My reason for going there was to have a look at the project and to give my support for a week.

It was a winter's day which, due to the geographical position high up in the interior of the country, meant that the temperatures were unbelievable, ranging from freezing or below at night to 18 or even 21 degrees Celsius during midday. It was amazing, freezing one minute and vaguely warm the next. I did not enjoy the weather at all because I was never quite sure what to dress for. One minute you were in a heavy coat, the next minute a T-shirt!

When I arrived for the first time at the Miracle House, I was shocked at the conditions of the home. The children lived in poverty, it was quite horrific. The project was situated in a big house in the town centre with no heating, no electricity, no hot water, no telephone, few windowpanes – even the floorboards were broken and the walls were in desperate need of a coat of paint. I had never seen such a rundown project. They had no money and they never even really knew where the next meal was going to come from. But the staff and children were a great contrast with the physical conditions of the project.

It was run by a black (so-called 'coloured' in South African terminology) husband and wife from the local township called Andy and Rose. Andy was familiar with hardships and struggle after being imprisoned for four years by the former apartheid government for political involvement. Here was a man with so much compassion that he had dedicated his life and that of his family to running this home for street children in a place where apartheid was still very evident and nobody was really interested in supporting him or the project. Andy and Rose and the forty wonderful children survived through prayer. They had no real social work help, no significant church support, no great donations coming in, and Andy and Rose shared everything that they had with the children who loved them both dearly, even calling Andy 'daddy'. The children ranged from age six to sixteen and, apart from having love and care and a roof overhead, still looked like street children with no new clothes ever arriving and the most minimal of facilities.

The children and staff were in desperate need of encouragement and that is exactly what I attempted to do in my time there – to encourage them in what they were doing and to try and help practically. They worked day in, day out, struggling for survival within a town of many rich people who turned a blind eye to them. In this type of situation one often feels inadequate to encourage such obvious saints, but it is important to realise that God has equipped each and every one of us to be able to encourage and to get involved practically even if we feel that we are not worthy. Sometimes just to be recognised and affirmed by someone from the outside gives heroes the strength to go on and if I could be of any help, whether practically or simply by encouraging, I was going to do my best to do it.

Of an evening the children used to sit snuggled up to one another next to an open fire to try to keep warm. They would all be in one room to keep the heat in, and it was at that time that I noticed the children and staff spending time with God. They would sing, pray, chat and joke together; it was truly an honour to be a part of. I had learned a few Xhosa songs during my Isaiah 58 days and we were able to swap songs with each other. We sang so much that I started to lose my voice which made the children sing even harder to carry my part. It was a great time as we sang harmonies together; another of those precious moments very similar to those of the early days of Isaiah 58. We then prayed together for the real day-to-day needs of the project like food, clothes and education. The children's effect on me was probably more encouraging to me than I could ever hope to be to them. Again, I was seeing destitute children finding peace and safety through nothing more than faith in God and his workers.

I played a lot of soccer with the kids who were

Typical street kids in East London, South Africa

Thulani

Durban street boys with their glue bottles

Escaping reality: Joseph inhales benzine from a sock

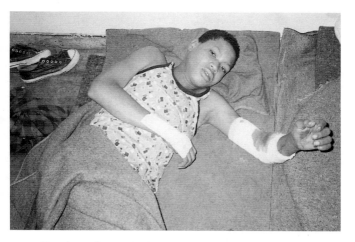

Boy in police cell after being mauled by police dog

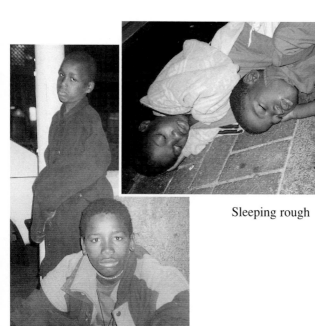

Sleeping rough

Hanging tough in Durban

Christmas 1997 at Daily Bread

Swimming practice with Pat Lottering and Tom

Auntie Maggie and children of Isaiah 58 Children's Village

Tom and Sinesipho from Isaiah 58

Survival on the rubbish dumps

Safety at Isaiah 58: Zanyiwe

Siphokazi and her baby Siphiwo enjoying their new lives

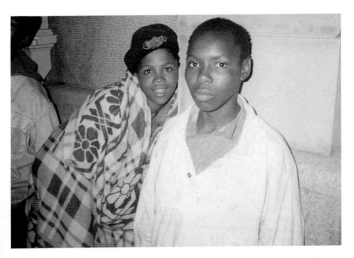

Felicia and Nomsa still on the streets of East London

Mduduza now living happily with his mother

Tom visiting the Isaiah kids in 1998

predominantly boys, and we spent much time simply 'hanging out', getting to know each other. I tried to organise as many recreational activities as I could for them. One day I arranged to take them to one of the local tourist attractions, a 'hot spring' where naturally hot water coming from a spring in the ground is used for swimming pools and even on the freezing days the water was fantastic and the steam would rise off the pools. The kids laughed and played. They were never usually taken out due to lack of transport and helpers. Andy loved it as it was a time for him to relax. I wanted to try and take the pressure off him for that week.

On a practical level I talked with Andy as to what the project really needed and two suggestions from him were electricity and a wall around the house for the children's safety. He was the expert who knew what was needed so I went back to Daily Bread in East London to sell the idea to the trustees. They agreed to help out and after a short wait a six-foot wall was built around the property, giving the children a safe playing area inside, and electricity was installed, opening a whole new world of lights, water, warmth and a little TV.

I kept up my relationship with Andy and Rose and the Miracle House the entire time that I was in East London, even though I did not get enough time to visit them much. Today not much has changed. They are still living in relative poverty and continue to live by faith. A few businesses in town have started donating food and other useful products. They battle on each day but every time I visit them the one thing that I notice is how much Andy and Rose love the children and how much the kids realise this. Despite lacking many material things they have a certain internal peace and such a humble attitude. Well, you would, wouldn't you, if you watched and recognised God's miracles every day?

In August 1998, I sent my Amos Trust volunteer Joe Walker to Miracle House from Durban to serve Andy and Rose for a week. He too was shocked at the poverty. Joe, who was certainly not a stranger to street children projects, was able to encourage and again take some of the pressure off Andy and Rose. In doing so, Joe had to rough it living at the project and he soon learnt what it was like to be freezing at night, to wash in freezing cold water and to live among rats and insects. Courageously, he admitted that it had been the hardest week of his life but possibly one of the most fulfilling. He had sacrificed personal comforts to encourage and support. He had felt completely out of his depth during the experience but also remembered in awe that Andy, Rose and the children lived there every day.

I want to keep my links with Miracle House in the future and, using Andy's list of needs, I have a few ideas of how to help. One possible future idea is to send perhaps ten volunteers from South Africa and perhaps the UK to paint the walls, mend the floors, fix the windows and tackle all the other parts of the building that need attention. However, such a team would not do this on their own but as a joint effort with the kids and under the close supervision of Andy and Rose. It would be a dual-purpose visit. They could fellowship with the children – encouraging them, listening to them and affirming them – but the volunteers would also be able to serve the project in a practical way.

My time at the Daily Bread project in East London was different from anything that I had been involved with previously. The first, most important difference was that the 'kids' were not all 'kids' there. Some of the 'young people' were as old as twenty-three. The boys aged fourteen and over lived on one farm and the girls of all ages and boys under the age of fourteen lived at another farm about 2 km away. The total number of 'young people' living at the project was two hundred with the capacity to take many more. In contrast to Miracle House, Daily Bread had plenty of support, plenty of vehicles, a social work system in place and a huge staff with central offices in town for the trustees.

What I tried to do as Director of Childcare at Daily

Bread was to install programmes which included recreation and fun activities, spiritual activities, everyday responsibilities and a team of people who could run this programme and eventually take over from me. It was an impossible task for one person. However, I was able to employ a man called Mike Nomtoto to work alongside me as my partner. Mike was a former boxer as well as a pastor in the International Assemblies of God Church and a journalist with the local newspaper. His arrival at the project was quite an amazing story. He had been driving past the farm and just felt the Lord telling him to go in and visit. He did so. We met and found that we shared many of the same ideals as Christians. Ultimately we became close friends as well as work colleagues.

Together we embarked on giving the children the loving care that they deserved, tried to turn their boredom into fun and to live among them as brothers to support them. Mike and I actually lived on-site at the project for quite some time. He would go home at weekends to be with his wife and children but sacrificed a lot by spending great amounts of time with the former street children at the project. Along the way we encountered many problems. Probably my first and hardest decision was to arrest two of the boys for raping one of the girls.

In the bush area between the two farms, two boys aged sixteen and eighteen had allegedly lured a 13-year-old girl to walk with them. In a quiet area with no one else around, they had then taken it in turns to rape her repeatedly. I was devastated when the news reached me of this vicious attack and I instantly called the boys into my office where I told them that I was going to arrest them. They did not try to resist and I drove them down to the police station in town. I did tell them that even though they must be punished and that I hated what they had allegedly done, I did not hate them and would continue to encourage and support them as the judicial system dealt with them. They were arrested and sent to prison where they awaited trial. Obviously I could not bail them because it would mean that they would have been in the company of the girl that they had allegedly raped. It was a difficult time as both of them were boys that I had been working with and both came from very difficult backgrounds, the youngest one particularly so having suffered horrific sexual abuse as a child.

The boys both sat in prison for six months and at the trial the older of the two boys escaped from the courtroom. It was an amazing moment. As we sat in the courtroom, I noticed him dart down the steps. As I looked around I realised that no one else had seen him. I suddenly heard a shout, presumably from a security guard, and then silence. The court was stunned and after a few tense moments a report was brought back to the court that the boy had escaped. Witnesses from the outside said that they just saw the boy run out of an open door and down the streets with security police chasing after him. However, he outran them.

This is not an uncommon scene in South Africa as the number of prisoners who actually escape from prison and from the courts on the days of their trial is absolutely staggering. Maybe that is why no one ever really worries when they get sentenced to life imprisonment. It seems as if there is a fairly good chance that they will escape.

I found the boy on the streets a few days later. He told me that while he was imprisoned the abuse was so unbearable that he could not go back there. As a first-time prisoner he was made 'girlfriend' to the other prisoners on different days of the week. They had also tattooed gang numbers across his chest and on his arms. I could not force him to go back to prison as he would not have agreed to that. I could not help but think that he had suffered greatly for what he had done. He asked me to say sorry to the girl that he had raped and asked me whether she was recovering from her injuries. He never returned to jail for that crime, but did get picked up for theft at a later stage (using a different name). Life was not quite as bad for him for that short spell in prison as he was not a first-time inmate in the eyes of the other prisoners.

The other boy received a suspended sentence for statutory rape as, despite the girl's testimony, they could not prove that the girl had not given consent. We did not however allow him back to the project.

Mike and I knew that we had to try and tackle the negatives and that one important aspect would be the children's sport and leisure as this is recognised worldwide as a fantastic means to keep kids and youth out of trouble. The boys already had a soccer team called 'Daily Stars' which played in the local league. We encouraged this and linked up with my good friend Patrick Lottering who gave some training advice. Results on the field were not always positive although they did manage to bring a trophy back after a championship in the local area. The boys were committed to the team and to training and this was one positive discipline that they already had.

Being a former boxer, Mike opened a gym for the boys. Boxing is traditionally one of the top sports in black South Africa. East London is seen as a Mecca for boxing with many world champions originating from this area. Even as I write this there are four world champions, most from the stable of Mzi Mguni, or 'Bra Mzi' as he is affectionately known by the community. The most famous of the champions is Vuyani 'the beast' Bungu who has defended his International Boxing Federation junior featherweight title over twelve times. Even Evander Holyfield on a recent trip to South Africa paid homage to boxing's South African Mecca by coming to East London and addressing a stadium full of fans in Mdantsane township. The boys from Daily Bread as well as the boys of Isaiah 58 were present and thrilled that day amid an excited crowd of people trying to get close to him when he arrived at East London Airport.

We then followed him to the Sisa Dukashe Stadium where he addressed his waiting fans.

Mike's gym at the project was very successful and many of the boys trained enthusiastically under Mike and his well-disciplined style. They used to train, spar and hold competitions on site at the project with local boxing clubs. Our boys were strong and street tough so they usually won. The boys were proud of their boxing and even convinced me to train with them, which I did. It was hilarious and I was a little unfit by boxing standards, to say the least. The lads were perfectly fit with not an ounce of fat and had highly defined six-packs. They used to run for miles around the local area dressed in heavy clothing and dustbin liners to make them sweat. Some even wore old wetsuits that they had found discarded. I, on the other hand, was certainly not in the same league and wasn't going to be the next Rocky. However, I gave it a try, minus the excessive roadrunning – you know, bad back and all that!

At first they started me on fitness training – an exhausting mixture of exercises ranging from skipping to dance-like exercises with sudden stomach-killers in between. I started to get fit slowly. My dancing didn't improve but I did lose a lot of weight and started to build up stamina. Soon it was time to start sparring. On my first attempt I tried to put as much 'gear' on as possible; head guard, gloves and most importantly the groin protector, ready for those loose upper cuts. My first try was against a 21-year-old called Vusumzi who did not consider himself a serious boxer and was just fooling around fighting me, the easy target. As we fought he landed a punch square on my nose, and anyone who has ever boxed will know that when you receive a clear punch to the face it is so infuriating that you start to lash out any way you can, which of course leaves you open to another attack. I decided that for my own pride I needed to land at least one punch and I lashed out in a completely undisciplined manner, missing hopelessly with my first two left jabs.

However, with no real aim I put all my weight and strength behind a right hook which miraculously connected with him straight in the head, sending him flying and dazed on to the floor. I panicked, saying, 'Sorry, *brah*! Hey, I didn't mean to hurt you' as I attempted to pick him up. He got up smiling but I did feel guilty, especially as it had been quite good fun knocking him for six and all the other lads were egging me on and howling with laughter. He was about half my size though!

My most serious attempt at proper sparring came against a lad called Lindile Mageu who was a very good boxing prospect and had the possibility of turning professional. I realised that he was going easy on me but after three rounds I was shattered. My lungs couldn't draw air fast enough, the pain was excruciating, I just could not go on. 'Water, I need water now!' I shouted, and as I stood to my feet for round four I could hardly get up. My opponent had run rings around me until I was reduced to an exhausted sweat-ball on the point of collapse. It took a while for my chest to recover as I sat there, unable to get to my feet. I could not go on and it was then I realised just how super-fit you have to be to be a boxer. I will always admire boxers for their fitness because I have tried it unsuccessfully. The boys laughed. It was great entertainment for them. I did continue to train with them for a while when I had the time but realised that I felt a lot happier and safer riding waves than standing in a ring.

The boys' competitions that they had with other projects were amazing. They started about 6 p.m. at night and ended at seven the next morning with about twenty fights having taken place. On one occasion I went the distance as a spectator, staying up until the last bout had finished. I think that most importantly the boys really started to feel that they existed and that the community took an interest in them.

We tried to encourage other sports, such as table tennis

and basketball. The Amos Trust donated funds for a full-size table tennis table which the kids loved. We even had table tennis championships which were great fun. I would arrange prizes for the winners and yet again we proved to have some very good quality players. The competitions themselves were very tough battles and very well spectated. Mike and I also became table tennis fanatics of about the same quality and used to dual relentlessly to try and beat each other, along with Sakhumzi, another member of staff, who was also a mean hand at table tennis.

With the time on site becoming much less boring, the children were beginning to change their behaviour. They were no longer getting arrested and fewer thefts took place on the farms. The dignity levels were also rising among the children, which gave rise in turn to a lot of good feeling at the project. Mike and I tried to increase the number of weekend excursions we gave the kids to make life a bit more interesting for them and to get them out of the farms where they lived and schooled.

With two hundred children at the project it was impossible to take everyone on an excursion in one go. We had to form a roster where some children would go on an excursion one week while the other children would perhaps watch videos or play games at the project, and the next week we would swap round. The children enjoyed trips to the beach, to the zoo, to play 'laser games' or to the cinema. Sometimes we would hold video evenings at the project, hiring a selection of movies for the kids to watch. This was one of their favourite activities.

At Christmas the children virtually lived at the beach. It is cheap and if well supervised a great day out. The girls would tend to go to Nahoon beach – a quiet, safe beach in East London – or to the swimming pools on the beachfront, as would the small boys. The older boys, however, were not interested in this and wanted to go to East London beachfront where the people would barbecue, party and have fun.

The lads would swim, relax and dance to the endless *kwaito* (local) music blaring out from parked cars and the notorious local beach cafe, 'Beachburger'. It was harmless fun. They always behaved and by the end of the day would be exhausted and ready to go home as would the staff and myself who also enjoyed these days but usually ended up shattered and sun-drenched.

Whenever a big event happened in East London I would try to get the children involved. One of the favourites was when the legendary soccer team, Kaizer Chiefs from Johannesburg, came to play at the Sisa Dukashe Stadium in Mdantsane. It was a great atmosphere at the match and I caused quite a lot of interest, being the only white face in the crowd. The fans were very friendly to me and I became the marker through which people spotted their friends. They would say, 'We are sitting just to the right of the whitey' and their friends would say, 'Oh, that's easy, then!' People that I had not seen for ages came and said 'Hi' after spotting me, and long-lost friends found me that day, saying, 'I spotted you from right over the other side of the stadium.'

Another time at the same stadium myself and thousands of Bafana Bafana (nickname for the South African National soccer team) fans gathered to watch, live via satellite, the game between South Africa and France in the 1998 World Cup finals. I kept my England shirt hidden under my jacket and watched from within the huge crowd. This time my beacon-like qualities were slightly dampened by the fact that it was a night event. It was great fun, if slightly shambolic as the electricity died halfway through the first half. I thought I was going to be in the middle of a riot. Fortunately, ten minutes into the second half the picture reappeared, not that it did much to cheer the crowd up as South Africa continued to play appallingly. Coming from England and familiar with a national team with possibly the worst luck in the world, I was able to sympathise.

Two things that I've noticed about being the only white

face at events in South Africa are, first, how everyone does their utmost to make you feel at home and, second, that there is always, *always* a drunk guy who stands by you, talking directly into your face for the entire event. It is like an unwritten rule, as if someone says, 'Quick! There is the white guy. Where's the drunk?' Everywhere I go, I am followed by this guy who changes in looks but keeps the same characteristics, each time suddenly becoming my best friend in the world as he unashamedly marvels at this strange sight and then standing so far into my personal space that I constantly find myself moving backwards to stop inhaling the liquor fumes. I love this guy but I do chuckle, wondering whether other people notice this man or whether they are so used to him that he goes unnoticed.

Obviously an overdose of fun times is just one way to help restore order, dignity and respect within the project. It does need to be equally balanced with rules, regulations and the instilling of responsibility and self-discipline. Mike and I sat down and designed the golden rules not only to restore law and order but also to restore morality. We banned substance abuse, drunkenness and introduced penalties for theft and acts of violence, and also gave guidelines for sexual morality, particularly in view of the AIDS epidemic in South Africa. It took time for the golden rules to sink in but slowly and eventually they started having effect. Level of mutual respect increased and the character of the girls particularly but also that of the boys changed dramatically. This period was a liberating time when the children were taught their importance and how to recognise and respect the importance of others. It was also a time when many of the children were able to come to staff members and explain their hopes, dreams, worries and fears in a healthy way.

Mike and I tried to encourage the children to explore their own spirituality. They knew that we both had personal faith in Jesus Christ and, after a while, through chatting openly with them and from attending a few church services a core of the boys decided to think about the implications of being a Christian and the Christian life. Mike being a pastor at the Bisho International Assemblies of God Church meant that the boys easily adopted a church base, not at all through force but simply through meeting the church members when they visited the project and from attending church social functions. Many of the boys attend church every Sunday and we attempted to launch a weekday Bible study to encourage them during the week. This was great. The boys would pray openly about life at the project and indeed started to rely on God. The boys started singing together as a gospel choir, even performing at the church in Bisho. Spiritual growth among the boys reintroduced them to the community and gave them personal identity.

Each of the houses at the project had a housefather to oversee it and we had written into the programme the time for 'chatting' with the housefather before the children slept. This chat was at the discretion of the children and housefather. It was a time to discuss issues of personal and spiritual growth with a housefather most of whom were Christian. One of the housefathers called Ezra was the youth president for the region at Mike's church, so he was a very good role model for the children. The housefathers were able to help bring the project under control but at the same time to liberate the children with a new lifestyle of love, care and personal attention. Each cottage had its own housefather, and each housefather then reported directly to Mike Nomtoto, the project manager.

With a structure in place I was able to use the first six months as a perfect opportunity to launch into productive street work again. I would guess that I brought in approximately forty new children during that time with a steady flow after that. Not every child stayed permanently. For some it was a bridge for them to get off the streets and into home life with their own family, but for others it became home. I just spread the news around streets about the new changes at Daily Bread and word of mouth did the rest. Soon the number of street children in East London had dropped to only a handful. Sometimes none could be found at all at night. Admittedly, as I mentioned before, it was a dual effort because if I did not get them off the streets and into the project it was only a matter of time until the police arrested them and imprisoned them for petty theft.

With all the new changes and the influx of new kids there was quite an air of excitement among the former street children of East London. Morale was high, activities were plentiful and all of the children were in full-time education at the government-run school that was based on site at the farm. This school had been running for quite some years with a bridging school to allow the children to catch up and a high school for the children once they progressed. Truancy rates at the school improved slightly but I must admit they always remained a problem.

We formed boys' and girls' committees to represent the views of the children in decision-making at the projects. This enabled the boys to realise that we wanted to run the projects and make decisions in the interest of the children. They felt that they now had a voice; however, every now and again the committees would step out of line, perhaps dealing out a punishment to another child instead of reporting the incident to us. We would then haul the boys in and deal with the situation straight away. Nobody was above the law!

With the work in full flow we were able to set up mechanisms of support for the children and indeed for street children in general. In some cases children who had been arrested for petty crime were also given hope. Sometimes I was able to intercept the process of them going to jail and bring them into the project under a court order by actually speaking with the prosecutor and judge or speaking for them in court. On one occasion I remember a concerned social worker phoning me to inform me of a young boy who was behind bars for petty theft and about to appear in court. I raced down to interview him in the cells. When I put the idea of the project to him he was obviously very relieved. The judge agreed to the idea and he came to live at the farm. This type of intervention is so much more humane than throwing him in an overcrowded cell with older inmates who would rape him and quite probably leave him HIV-positive.

South Africa is a dangerous country and although they live safely most of the time sometimes the children at the projects can encounter difficulties. Mike and I found that we often had to be a support to children from our project who had fallen victim to different types of violence on home visits or visits to the local townships.

On one occasion one of our 15-year-old girls, Phumla, was raped after having been enticed to abscond and visit one of the local townships by another girl. She was abducted by a taxi-driver as she endeavoured to return to the farm. The taxi-driver led her off to his shack where he forced her inside, beating her up severely, raping her and leaving her for dead. She crawled through the bush and across a small stream to the next area of housing, where she was spotted by some kind community members who took her in while one of them ran to the police station. After I had been driving around looking for Phumla, we got a call that night at the farm from the police to say that they had found her and that she had been raped. It is a dreadful moment when you hear news like that about someone you care for and automatically I switched into override 'get the job done' mode so as not to be ineffective. I drove out to Duncan Village where she had been found. She was battered and bruised with a heavily beaten face, her hand was puffed up with a bite mark and her body had signs of being beaten with a stick. She was in shock, lying on a bed that the kind helpers had put her on. Phumla had not said much until I appeared, but as I entered the room she called out my name and then lay down again with perhaps at least the knowledge that she had been found by her 'family'. She could not walk, and I tried to pick her up to get her into the police vehicle which took her to the hospital. It is a devastating experience for her that will be with her for the rest of her life. It would be very wrong of me to think that I could understand the trauma that she had been through but I wanted desperately to try and help her. Even if I couldn't take the pain away or turn back the clock, I was determined to do something.

I tried to be as much of a support to Phumla as possible after the ordeal. The housemother at the girls' farm, a Christian woman called Nosimo Kantyo, was the one who was really able to counsel her and empathise. I just tried to be there whenever they called. I also handled the following of the police investigation. The police had horrific evidence of brutal rape from the doctor's examination immediately after the attack. They also had recovered semen belonging to the rapist and all that they needed now was the rapist himself. Finding him was like looking for a needle in a haystack; that is, of course, unless you have faith in God, who has an amazing way of showing his absolute power and love for the oppressed at the strangest of times!

I took Phumla back to the police station where they took her to identify the man's shack but he was nowhere to be seen and seemed to have moved on. We were down-hearted. I decided just on the off-chance to visit the taxi ranks where hundreds of taxis come in and out each day. As we arrived there I noticed about twenty taxis. However, before I could even finish contemplating the impossible situation the girl shrieked, 'That's the taxi!' as she pointed excitedly to a blue taxi parked at the rank. I must admit I was sceptical. There were many blue taxis that all looked the same. How on earth could the first taxi that we see be the one? I drove past, shielding her as she peered around me. She was convinced that that was the one. I stopped about 50 metres away and wrote down the registration number, phoned the police and observed.

The police must have been busy as they took quite some time to arrive and unfortunately as we waited I noticed that the taxi pulled off. I could not believe it. Phumla was now able to identify the driver as well, so we started to follow, two cars behind. The girl and I were both really excited but careful not to be seen. I phoned the police again from my mobile phone, they then phoned me back and stayed on the line. I kept them updated on my exact position and they tracked us. After about ten minutes they were behind our vehicle and overtook. I pointed the taxi and the driver out to them and dramatically they swooped on him, cutting off his passage forward. I sped up, cutting off any possibility of him reversing, and the girl jumped out with me and identified the man to the police. The rapist remained motionless, dazed and probably shocked at being caught but showing no emotion. A huge crowd gathered, guessing the situation, and all cheered in support of the girl. Phumla was quite proud to be a part of actually catching the rapist. In a strange way it was therapeutic for her to have actually helped in the arrest and especially to know now that he would be behind bars. The police led away the man who had robbed the girl of her dignity. He was locked up to await trial. We drove back to the project where Nosimo couldn't believe the good news. Catching the rapist doesn't take away the pain and hurt. Only counselling, love and care and God's unique comforter, the Holy Spirit can do that in time, but at least it was a step in the right direction.

My time at Daily Bread was very different to anything that I had been involved with before. It was in a sense dreaming the impossible dream because it was such a vast project. The project now has over 250 young people. Mike is still involved as the manager. Both Mike and I encountered untold hardships during our work there ranging from extreme burn-out to persecution for changing the status quo. It was a magical time of camaraderie and joy with the staff and children. The character of the children changed dramatically and their faith in God was discovered and nurtured. They were now strong enough to stand up for their rights and continue in the same manner. They now had hope, a supportive staff team and church, and had experienced a most joyous period at the project. Life had changed for the children of Daily Bread.

8   A life on the dumps

Overseas visitors have been particularly shocked when seeing a whole community living on East London's rubbish dump. I spent a fantastic week getting to know various crew members of the *Anastasis* mercy ship, a Christian medical ship travelling round Africa. I had been hugely impressed at the practical and medical implications of a ship such as this, dedicated to offering often expensive medical treatment to some of the poorest communities in the world. The ship was full of people from different countries around the world. These Christians dedicated a year or more to the work and their vibrancy and commitment was incredible. I found the young people to be a real encouragement and many of them expressed the desire to see the real South Africa. I remember especially the Dutch guys being particularly interested in spending time in the townships.

After meeting the former street kids and tip kids at Isaiah 58 they asked me if they could see where these children came from. As it happened, that day there was a donation of bread that I had to take to the community on the rubbish dumps and I decided that they could come with me; there were about eight of them.

We loaded the pick-up truck with the *Anastasis* crew, a handful of Isaiah 58 children and a large bread donation, and drove down the approach road to the tips past the familiar armed security guards to the crowds of locals scratching through the rubbish that had most recently been dumped. When the people realised that there was fresh bread coming they hurriedly congregated around our vehicle; a crowd of more than fifty swamped it. I got out of the truck. Some of the crew members remained in the front of the cab, the others were in the back helping with the distribution. With some of the local youth we attempted to organise an orderly queue but we soon realised that this was going to be impossible. The bread was fresh, the people were hungry and it was plain to see that there was not going to be enough to go around. The crowd was volatile and in desperation. Some of the youths who I knew well had mobilised themselves to help keep order and they, myself and some of the Isaiah children had to physically form a human chain and press ourselves against the crowd to keep them back while the *Anastasis* crew members handed out the loaves. The situation became tense and the crew were wide-eyed and frightened. I just prayed that no one would draw a knife or a gun. With all our strength we held the crowd off until the loaves had been distributed. I then quickly dived into the truck and pushed my way out of the crowd. The youths from the tips were lashing out at anyone, trying to grab on to the truck in desperation. The *Anastasis* crew members were visibly shaken by the experience. As I pulled off I thanked the youths for their help, but they just laughed as if it was all in a day's work. Those from the *Anastasis* who had witnessed the events of the day had been greatly impacted by what they saw and left with a small insight into community life and the desperation of the rubbish dumps, no doubt very different to the community that they had come from. I'm sure when they arrived back in Isaiah 58 they were able to appreciate just how much the little ones had suffered who had grown up on a rubbish dump.

The Second Creek refuse tip is the East London municipal rubbish dump tucked away out of sight in a part of the black and coloured township called Parkside. It's a large area about the size of perhaps a large soccer stadium and is the place at which the rubbish from the whole of greater East London is dumped. The short-sighted and prejudiced

town-planners from the old regime saw fit to put the
rubbish dumps in an area inhabited by non-whites and
therefore out of sight from the pretty white areas. What was
created through this was a community of the poorest of the
poor living on the fringes of and sometimes literally on the
rubbish dump itself. Today, impoverished people scavenge
daily, eking out an existence amid the rubbish of the rich,
often eating their rotten left-overs and attempting to sal-
vage their waste.

There are some thousand people living at the Second
Creek refuse dump; most of them live in tiny shacks to the
side of the designated tip area, among the rubbish. There is
no running water except from a few taps nearby and no
toilet facilities – people simply have to do their business in
the bushes. Often, after the initial shock of the rotten, foul
smell as it hits you on entering rubbish dumps, one of the
first things that you notice is how many young children you
can see. They are everywhere, playing among the rubbish,
helping their mothers pick through the waste, eating rotten
food and waiting eagerly for the familiar truck coming from
the local sweet factory to dump its waste.

Children are literally born into rubbish. They are dressed
in filthy rags, and what is clearly visible is the amount of
skin sores and scars on their bodies. Their heads are usually
roughly shaven as this is the only way of keeping the lice
from becoming unbearable, and almost all of the children
also have lice on their bodies and often catch scabies.
Worms is a problem that affects all the children. There
are many different types of worm but the most common one
that I have seen can often be up to a metre long inside the
child and comes out whole when the child is given worm
syrup. Other types of worm can affect the brain and cause
the child to have fits and, if not treated, the child can
eventually die.

The children play obliviously alongside the rubbish. After
all, it is probably all that they know. They learn from a very

young age how to fend for themselves by scavenging. The dumps are profoundly unhealthy places, not least of all as they are a breeding-ground for disease. Most children suffer from many of the various different ailments at one time or another including TB, skin diseases, lice, worms and of course HIV. There are good local clinics that the people can go to but the sheer volume of people means that no matter what ailment they have, they would have to walk to the clinic, and wait most of the day to eventually get treated. Most of the diseases from the tips can be treated if caught early enough.

AIDS, however, is a different story and indeed poses a huge problem on the rubbish dumps. There are many contributing factors to the AIDS crisis in the tips area many of which will be apparent as this chapter progresses, but the sheer volume of abuse – not to mention the lack of moral standards caused and fuelled by the lack of self-love – within the community has a major impact. You can see it everywhere. The combination of AIDS, disease, alcoholism and poverty takes its toll and leaves the people looking depressed, thin, weary and desperately unhealthy. In theory AIDS could wipe out the tip community, but I'm sure that if this is the case even more desperately poor people would soon fill their empty spaces, as the poverty itself is so vast.

Medical waste has been found at the dump on a number of occasions, including blood samples, medicines, used syringes and needles. This comes straight into the hands of playing children. Everybody lives for today at the rubbish dumps because tomorrow may never happen. Long-term planning does not exist. Life is short; death is everywhere, inevitable and therefore ignored. It is indeed the saddest place I have been to in my life. Babies are born into rubbish, doomed from their conception.

I remember very clearly one afternoon at Isaiah 58. I was unloading a donation from the pick-up truck when I noticed a man crawling in through our gates. My initial thoughts were that the man was drunk, then I soon realised that this was not the case. I could see that he had quite a serious injury, he had obviously been stabbed. We pulled him inside the gates and I phoned for an ambulance immediately. As he lay there I could see his insides coming out through a gaping hole in his side, just above his stomach, about three inches across. The man was also high on benzine, but nevertheless was in significant pain. I knew the man; he was a tip dweller who was starting to spend more and more of his time on the East London streets. He was also a habitual benzine-sniffer and was so affected by this habit that it even affected the way he walked. He could not control his body properly, it was as though it had affected his nervous system. The man, who was approximately twenty-two years old, regularly sat outside shops in town begging for small change. Most of the time he was so high that most people thought he was crazy but sometimes I would catch him sober and find a soft, real person hiding inside, and whether high or sober he was never violent.

The ambulance arrived and they quickly got to work on the young man. Before long they had him bandaged up. This was obviously a familiar sight to them. If I heard them correctly it had been his spleen hanging out of the hole, but I could be wrong there! I think they bandaged him up primarily to stop the bleeding and they then rushed him to hospital. What was interesting about the whole event was the fact that the man had used Isaiah 58 as his sanctuary, literally crawling up from the tips. It was certainly an eye-opener for me. Even though I had seen many stab wounds on the streets none had been quite as bloody and graphic as this one. I had to laugh the next day because later that evening I saw the man hobbling around in town, high once again. Maybe a stab wound like that was just no big deal!

The dump community is the lowest rung on the social ladder. Many of the tip inhabitants have simply given up on life and on trying to achieve anything. Years and years of struggle have given rise to the notion that they are not really worth much and certainly will never achieve anything significant in society. When a person gives up on the social requirements of life it often leads not only to a lack of self-value but also to complete disregard to the rights of others living around them and indeed a disregard for human life. Existing amid the rubbish, people begin to be treated like rubbish by others. Their self-esteem is so low that in their own minds they start to value their lives and the lives of others as just that: rubbish. This whole equation makes the tips the most dangerous area in greater East London. Lawlessness often rules and life is simply not worth much.

The main cause of this is alcohol. What little money is made through scavenging is invariably spent on cheap alcohol to escape from the horrors of life. This has had a tremendously damaging effect, particularly on the women and children living on the tips. The children are soon abused by drunk parents or members of the community and become particularly vulnerable to rape. When we asked some of the women living at the Second Creek squatter camp about the situation of abuse in the community, one of them simply said, 'We get raped, often. That is life here.'

Almost all the women have at one time or another been raped at the dumps and young girls growing up there become the most vulnerable to falling victim to this abuse. Men and women alike rely on cheap alcohol or drugs to survive and escape the horror and perhaps because of this there have been hundreds of murders on the rubbish dumps, and even the police and Fire Brigade are too scared to venture into the tips at night.

There are many gangsters living on the tips who terrorise the community armed with guns, knives and bushcutters and will not think twice about killing anybody who crosses them. They make slightly more money than the others by selling marijuana and by breaking into shops and houses in town or by stealing pigs and goods from around the local area. These gangsters are able to rape women, knowing that it is unlikely that anyone will try and stop them; they would perhaps kill anyone who intervened. The gangsters congregate in different areas of the rubbish dumps constantly smoking marijuana and drinking cheap alcohol. They control the whole area through violence.

In 1995 a group of gangsters was running amok on the tips. They were wild and out of control. Gunfire would ring out every night and the tips would be ablaze with burning shacks, usually those of people who had stood up against the gangsters. Isaiah 58 is situated right next to the rubbish dumps so at this time I had a view of the whole area and remember standing watching burning shacks and listening to gunfire, wondering who was dying. One particularly crazy night the sky was alight and shots rang out wildly, sirens rang in the distance. A 4-year-old girl who was living at Isaiah 58 started crying. She had lived on the tips and was in tears because she thought that it might be her mother or father who were burning to death in the flames. I comforted her and took her inside, knowing that a report on the goings on would emerge only in the morning. The little girl and her 8-year-old brother had been rescued from the rubbish dumps a few months earlier. The next day we learned that their father, who I knew well and had in fact become a Christian recently, had stood up against the gangsters and had been shot dead. His house had also been burned down – it was tragic. A week later there was a pauper's funeral for him, the cheapest funeral possible, as he was one of the poorest of the poor. After a few days he was forgotten on the tips, but not in the hearts of his two grieving children.

One of the highlights for the children and indeed the adults of the rubbish dumps is when the waste arrives from the local sweet factory. This sounds like quite a pretty picture – children waiting for the sweets to arrive – but the reality is much more sinister. Of course, the attraction is not solely in eating sweets. It is in selling the sweets, so much so that it is not uncommon for people to be murdered by others as they try to get into the truck first. Many a child or adult has lost their lives as the sweet truck comes in, either through being murdered or by falling under its huge wheels. The children and young men wait at the gates for the lorry to arrive and when it does there is a mad scramble to jump on to it, holding on to just about any part of the vehicle they can. Just recently, another boy was squashed by the vehicle. There have been a handful of boys killed in this manner during my time in the area.

The children of the rubbish dumps grow up seeing the most horrific scenes. Children tell stories of watching people murdered, shot or perhaps stabbed. One child I spoke to told of watching a 17-year-old pregnant mother beaten to death by her brother who had made her pregnant. Others tell stories of finding dead bodies on the tips with their throats cut or dead babies abandoned among the rubbish.

Children play during the day and lie wide awake at night hiding under a blanket, praying that no one will remember that they are there. They live in fear. If children actually make it into their teens they are so heavily traumatised that they usually sink into the same lifestyle. In fact, many of the children are committing crimes themselves. They start by breaking into shops, houses or cars and indeed by the ages of sixteen or seventeen some have committed murders or rape already. I knew a 14-year-old boy who had grown up in the rubbish dumps. He had subsequently gone to the streets and met up with a group of street children. One of the street girls who was aged thirteen at the time asked him to murder another girl, which he did, and they hid her body in a sewerage drain. The rumour is that this boy has been involved in other murders since. It's hardly surprising, growing up in a place like the rubbish dumps. Many young girls have had back street abortions, some by the most horrific methods including physically beating the baby from the outside. Others drink a concoction that will kill the baby. How do children survive in such conditions with such degenerate social norms? Well, they run to the clean city streets to live in relative safety, or so they think.

Some people from the surrounding areas do try and set up initiatives to help the tip dwellers, but it has proved very difficult to establish lasting programmes due to the severity of the problems, lack of support, local politics and the danger upon entering the area. There are some dedicated people tirelessly running soup kitchens in local churches, taking their left-overs of food down to the community or perhaps running crèches for the small children. Others who have tried initiatives have given up and resorted to preaching only. It is as if even the Christians have given up on these people ever having any quality of life so they resort to 'getting them saved before they die'. Do not get me wrong, the gift of salvation is the greatest gift anybody can ever have. I guess I just feel that we as human beings have created environments like these and should therefore take responsibility to love and serve the communities in a way that will help these people discover God's love and salvation. But the tips are such volatile places that most potential do-gooders feel that they are taking a great risk going on to them. Indeed, would-be helpers have been mugged and some people dumping waste have been stabbed to death. Most kind-hearted donors will not actually venture on to the tips; they will wait at the entrances calling the people to them to receive donations. They are perhaps not unwise to do this.

The rubbish dumps are visually fascinating, they are emotive and challenging. It is the real face of poverty. So graphic are the pictures taken there that after seeing them most visitors who have come to stay with me have wanted to go down to the tips just to witness the sights for themselves. I do not think that this is necessarily some sort of romanticised voyeurism, simply wanting to taste a completely helpless situation from the comfort of a car or at least with someone who knows the people. Rather I think that seeing the sheer hopelessness and desperation of the rubbish dumps suddenly puts people in touch with the often hidden, compassionate creature instilled in us by God, usually masked by our seemingly insatiable appetite for materialism and self-absorption.

Depending on the level of openness of the individual observing the tips, two categories emerge. First are those whose response is in the 'Boy, this was a bad idea coming here. I'm terrified, let's get the hell out of here, this is not for me' category. These people invariably never come within a few miles of the tips again, eradicate any notion of compassion for the community living there and spend the rest of their lives telling the story of how dangerous and out of control the area is and how disgraceful the community was. They never really allow themselves to get to grips with understanding the complex situation.

One day I went to the rubbish dumps with the purpose of shooting a video to send back to the UK to show people, telling the story of the tip community and how Isaiah 58 had become involved with the children of the rubbish dumps. This is not something I particularly enjoy because I feel that it may not be the most tactful way of empathising with the community, shooting a video of the poorest of the poor in their misery. Fortunately, the local community members that I knew were very supportive as they knew that Isaiah 58 was a means of survival for many of their children. A person came with me on the trip who will remain nameless, let's just say that he came from an extremely different background from that of the tip community. As we entered the tips he started to panic. He became extremely nervous and started to deeply regret coming down. I'm sure he was thinking, 'Whose stupid idea was this?'

In the distance a fight broke out between two guys. Although this had nothing to do with us in the slightest, this incident was the last straw for him so I left him in the vehicle while I chatted to some of the locals, for he certainly wasn't about to get out of the car. I was slightly annoyed because the people who had greeted us that day had shown us nothing but friendship. He had been fearful of leaving his comfort zone, he had not allowed himself to look with compassion at the situation and receive the gift that they had to offer him.

The second category thankfully are the ones who arrive on the dumps and remain open. They are those who respond, saying, 'I have never seen such poverty, this is deeply moving, I have so much and yet . . .' These people go away feeling challenged personally. They often feel helpless but are determined to do something somewhere to serve the poor.

Occasionally, some visitors find the experience extremely emotionally disturbing. This is particularly true when one tries to grasp the concept that life amid the rubbish is for these people as real as our often safe, comfortable and comfortingly familiar lives are to us. Such people want to meet the community, chat with the kids and help in the least paternalistic way possible. Their lives are changed and often they are ready to allow their spirituality to be challenged as they take up one of the most fundamental parts of the Christian faith, fighting for social justice. I say this because if we truly want to emulate, imitate and model ourselves on the life of Jesus Christ then being dedicated to social action is essential.

Isaiah 58 was not initially started as a project for street children. It was opened by an East London dentist who, while feeding the people of the dumps, had been so moved by the plight of the children there that he decided he would open a home for them. It was in a sense a refuge for the children in danger on the rubbish dumps. The very nature of its location, right next to the dumps away from the shacks, made it a realistic place of safety for the children without removing them from their community or cutting their ties with their families. Due to the potential in size and a big crossover between tip kids and street kids it was natural after a while to extend hospitality and care to the greater population of street children. I must admit that when I arrived at Isaiah 58 in 1993 I did not realise that it had not been essentially a street children project. This misconception changed the very nature of the project over the next three and a half years.

Essentially, the children of the tips under the age of six years are the potential future children of the streets and flirting with street life begins as early as five or six. Becoming a fully fledged street child can often happen as early as eight or nine but usually at about ten or eleven. Obviously the horrific life on the tips sends the kids in search of a better life. It is certainly true to say that if a person really wanted to understand the street children of East London then to have at least some knowledge about Second Creek rubbish dumps is essential. Not all street children in East London come from the rubbish dumps but most of the dump children flirt with street life at some point and it is sad that, for some, street life with all its horrors is better than life at home.

Between 1993 and 1996 what we tried to do at Isaiah 58 was to identify the worst case kids at the rubbish dumps and to work with their parents to try and formulate a way of helping them. In essence we could offer a 'safe house' for the children to live in with a place to go to school or pre-school. Of course, the key ingredients of the project are love and care.

I first met Aya when he was three years old. His mother was a 20-year-old girl, already a heavy drinker, who had herself grown up on the tips and was very much a victim of tip life. She would scavenge on the tips with Aya's grandmother who was an alcoholic too. Almost every time I saw Aya's mother she was drunk, whether it be during the morning on the tips or later in the evening at her shack next to the dumps. The result of years of suffering combined with escapism through drinking had turned her into a social wreck. She looked twice her age, was thin and was often in trouble for theft and even violence. On one occasion she stabbed Aya's cousin who was fourteen at the time, and left her paralysed for a while. Aya was left to fend for himself most of the time or to play among rubbish while his mother scavenged. He would eat the rotten food provided by his mother when she was sober enough, and otherwise he ate whatever he could find. At three years old, Aya had very little real parental guidance and was becoming a prime target for disease and abuse. He was very thin with a huge pot-belly – a familiar sign in malnourished children. He was very small for his age with sores and worms. It was a tragic situation because he did not seem to stand a chance of surviving.

The shack that Aya lived in with his mother, his grandmother, his sister, his mother's sisters and their boyfriends was situated just off to the side of the rubbish dumps. His older sister and cousins had fled the area because of abuse, had become street children and taken to prostitution in town. I had taken one of his cousins out of street life and into Isaiah 58. Subsequently, I was able to work with the family and had got to know the boy's mother very well. The more time I spent monitoring Aya, the more that I realised that he was not simply a child at risk but also a child suffering great personal neglect as well as the neglect of his basic rights as a child.

Aya's cousin had been one of the most unmanageable street children I had known and the family could not believe how much she had changed through being at Isaiah 58. She was eleven years old. When I visited the family I spoke to them about the possibility of helping Aya, to try and save him from having to go down the same road which almost always led to the streets. They were thrilled because even though the family was suffering daily and had given up on any aspirations that they may have had, they saw hope in their offspring and still deeply loved them even if the rigours of their lives made it difficult for them to show this. I remember when I used to visit the family at their shack. Aya would see me coming down the pathway and would make a spirited dash and jump into my arms. I couldn't help but build up quite a close relationship with him so it was not a difficult step for me to remove him from the rubbish dump and take him to Isaiah 58 about half a mile away. His mother was in full agreement and was encouraged to visit as much as possible, of course she had to be sober if she wanted to visit him. Aya started his new life along with an older sister who was eight at the time and his older cousin who was already there.

Aya, like most other tip kids, adapted easily to Isaiah 58 where there were many familiar faces. His physical needs were attended to. He had worms, head lice and fungal infections on his scalp and body, with sores that were not healing. All his infections were treated and with his new healthy diet at Isaiah 58 he progressed rapidly, filled out and after a while even his pot-belly started to slowly decrease in size. Eventually Isaiah 58 had about twenty little ones aged between four and seven rescued from the rubbish dumps and the project became a real mechanism of support for that community.

Sometimes we had to be careful when admitting children to Isaiah 58. Some parents who were not living in hopeless circumstances would come to try and get rid of their kids, as if Isaiah 58 was some sort of boarding-school where they could leave their children, enabling them to drink and shed the responsibility of parenthood. We stood vehemently against this, insisting that Isaiah 58 was a place concerned with supporting desperate families, not breaking families up.

We recognised also that the whole tip community needed support – not just the children – and to enable us to really keep support mechanisms going for the families we used to donate food that we had received that could not be used at Isaiah. We would often get waste foods, in perfect condition, in volumes that were too big to use solely at Isaiah 58. So Auntie Maggie, the children and myself would load the pick-up truck and take the food to the tips and hand it out to the people. The children, in effect, were feeding their own families in the community. It was great because it taught them how to serve their own community, one of the most important things that they could learn.

There has been talk in recent years of the local council closing Second Creek refuse dump. I'm not sure quite what effect this would have on the tips community but obviously it would take away what little source of income they have. It is a difficult problem to try and solve primarily because it is essentially a creation of the apartheid era which has over time produced a community that lives in an extremely unnatural environment. Should the tips be closed, so that the tips community becomes just another squatter area? Perhaps what needs to happen is an improvement in the amenities and facilities in the area; for example, putting in toilets, running water, electricity and street lights. However, there is no quick solution to the problem. Initiatives will be needed to ensure that each child is able to attend school, proper social services will be needed to cater for children in danger and adequate policing will also be vital to try and reduce the levels of violence. The greater East London community needs to take responsibility for the community of people who have been living off their rubbish. While it was not the present government that created this mess I believe that the government of today needs to lead the way in the process of interaction and support for the community of Second Creek rubbish dump. Together with the community, the government must find a solution to the problem, if only for the sake of the children.

9 Mduduza: A story of new hope

Working with street children is certainly a rewarding vocation. The mere fact of serving children who are so close to
the heart of God brings times of extreme joy. However, the
nature of the work means also emotional and physical
vulnerability to the struggle of the streets. Sometimes kids'
lives are destroyed, sometimes they go back to the streets; it
does not always work out. I have seen many awful situations on the streets and sometimes it really breaks my heart.
Sometimes I break down and weep.

The reason that I often refer to the stories of children who
have been rescued from the streets as stories of hope rather
than success stories is because at the end of the day the
children's lives continue once the book is finished. These
children have an experience of being further along the road
to successful integration back into their society; in other
words, the hope is more evident.

Because things can go wrong, I would encourage anyone
with faith to pray for each child mentioned in this book.
Many people in the UK and in South Africa have prayed
continuously for children like Felicia and Nomsa and a girl
called Siphokazi who we will hear about later. There are
those children whose struggle with the streets continues,
hope appears, then is dashed. Sometimes I find myself
thinking, 'Lord, this is a hopeless situation. This child will
never survive, it's gone too far.'

However, I know that no matter how far a child has
deteriorated, God can make a way. It is important to
remember that God never gives up on us, so where do
any of us have the right to give up on a child?

Mduduza Zungu is an example of a life of endless struggle. He is a child who is close to my heart and I feel that God has brought us together for a reason. Yet I have had to ask myself, will his struggle ever end? Will he be free – free from the addiction to glue, free from the abuse of the streets, free to live the life God planned for him? There have been times when I have felt like giving up on him and times that he has given up fighting, but the Lord has carried on the struggle to set him free.

At fourteen Mduduza looks at least two years younger. His body is thin, dirty, marked with all the signs of the streets. His hair is dry, his head is scarred leaving patches without hair. His skin pulls tightly over his prominent cheekbones as he draws deeply from an old plastic milk bottle filled with glue as if that were his lifeline. After each draw he looks up; his eyes drowsy, lazy and lifeless. His skin is dry from lack of moisture and his feet tell the story of street life, always on the move, often on the run. He wears a red T-shirt, filthy, stained with city grime that has dulled its colour. The neck is stretched, leaving it hanging lop-sided on him; it is much too big. He wears a coat, again huge, somebody's throw away, which has become grey from the streets but may once have been a nice white coat. His trousers are held up by string; the zip is broken, the legs are far too long and he folds them unsuccessfully to stop himself tripping up. His wounded, marked, dry hands with filthy fingers clutch at the glue bottle. His hands are thin, almost skeletal as are his feet; his whole body shows that he has spent a major part of his life living on the streets.

He has seen it all, living among rapists, murderers, prostitutes, abusers, drunkards and, of course, his fellow street children. He has been sniffing glue day in, day out, for many years and it is taking a heavy toll upon him. His rationality is being lost, the ability to make decisions is waning. Logic is being lost to glue and it appears that he has given up, but I'm not so sure. Inside I see a desperate child,

clutching at anything. Often he cries out. I've seen it, I've
seen him crying irrationally, sleeping outside my flat, waiting hours until I notice him. I've seen him trying to
rationalise his emotions and giving up because the strength
of the glue just won't allow him to think properly. He just
starts to cry. His tears say it all: he wants hope yet he is at
that point of despair where he feels he has nowhere to turn.

In November 1996 I visited Durban for a week to explore
and research the street children on its city streets. I arrived
with Amos Trust volunteer Joe Walker and one of the first
things that we did was to take a walk around the streets. We
became very friendly with Mduduza and the group of
children that lived around the Point Road area near the
beach. Mduduza's friends were between the ages of ten and
fifteen, and their names were Thulani, Phiwenkosi, Thulani
(another one!) and Xolani. One of the things that surprised
me was how much they relied on glue to survive; they
sniffed openly. East London was not quite as open as this,
the street children were not so heavily involved with and
reliant on glue. We played soccer with these boys at night,
and during the day they would come with us to town or to
the beach or would simply sit chatting to us on the streets.
They really enjoyed the week as did Joe and I, and when the
time came for us to depart we took photos of each other and
said our farewells. Foolishly, I promised that I would come
back, thinking that I would be back within a few months,
not knowing that this would not happen. They wanted to go
back with us to East London but of course this was an
impossibility.

After the trip I really felt that God had shown these
children to us for a specific reason and I assumed that it
would be to help them in the near future. However, I was
very wrong about assuming the timing. I did not get back to
Durban for nearly two years. I had not realised that I would
have to spend a few months back in the UK sorting out my
work permit and, second that I would have to work again in

East London for about eighteen months after that. I had thought that I was going back to Durban and throughout the waiting period in the UK I had thought that my arrival back in South Africa would lead me straight back into Durban. When I returned to East London the weeks turned into months and it became apparent that I would not be back straight away.

Throughout this time I used to pray for each of these boys individually. Indeed one of the pictures that I took of these boys as we chatted on the beachfront in Durban became very familiar to Amos Trust supporters. It is a picture of the boys sitting huddled together, sniffing glue. It is a desperate picture, yet their beautiful eyes penetrate through to the heart of those who see the picture. To me, it signified a group of boys waiting for me in Durban, and it was a photo that I really cherished.

I returned to Durban for a couple of days in April 1998 with my sister Abi for a short holiday. Although we had a wonderful time, my attempts to locate the boys were fruitless. In June 1998, when I met with my father in Durban for a father-to-son heart-to-heart, I was unsuccessful when looking for these boys. However, when in July 1998 I finally moved to Durban permanently, I got to know all of the street children very quickly and soon found out that these boys were still alive, were still living in the streets but hadn't been seen for a little while. They were somewhere on Durban's streets and I was determined to find them.

One morning I saw a group of street kids. I recognised a few of them from the last few weeks of getting acquainted. As I greeted them across the street, they rushed over to me. One boy moved over to me, began to ask me for some small change and as he did so he looked up at my face, stopped in his tracks in disbelief and shouted, 'It's you!' Mduduza then launched himself toward me, hugging me like he might hug a family member when reunited. He then promptly burst into tears and said, 'I waited for you, Tom. You said you would come back.'

I was thrilled to see him yet felt awful that I had promised my return, given him hope and had not been able to follow through on it. It was then that I saw just how much the children hold on to hope. I had let him down.

I found out that during those two years Mduduza had lived mostly on the streets. He had made an attempt to go home and it had been successful until he stole the equivalent of sixty-five pounds from his father and ran back to the streets. He slipped straight back into street life and when I met him again I noticed quite a small but significant change in him. In 1996 he had been slightly more emotionally in control. I felt that the heavy glue abuse was starting to take its toll on his life. He no longer had the capacity to survive the streets; the streets were overtaking him, leaving him as a casualty. He would cry at the slightest misunderstanding. As I began to spend more time with him it became apparent that he was a walking time bomb, a victim of the streets, perhaps in his final stages of survival.

Mduduza's hope in me appeared to be all he had. I was amazed that in two years he had hardly grown at all, he just seemed a little thinner. He began to wait endlessly outside my flat, sometimes asleep on the pavement being stepped over by passers-by. At other times he would just sit, sniffing glue. He was making a very loud, clear statement to me that he was desperate and needed help. He wanted to meet me every day and if I was ever busy he would suffer rejection. I started making inquiries as to the whereabouts of his parents and found out that he had a mother who lived in a township called Lamontville, and a father who lived in another township on the other side of Durban called Inanda. The problem seemed to be that the mother was living in poverty so Mduduza had gone to stay with his father due to the fact that he was working in a factory. The father had taken another wife, which proved problematic for Mduduza as his stepmother treated him very badly. This situation forced him to look elsewhere, so he fled to the streets.

As I chatted to Mduduza I saw that he really loved his mother and wanted to live with her but knew that she was too poor and that he couldn't survive there. He was also worried about his father and what he would say to him about the money that he had stolen. I thought and prayed about the situation and decided I would try to reunite him with his mother. Obviously this would have financial implications because if I simply took him back home without considering this, it would be only a matter of hours before he came back to the streets. The problem with his father would be fairly easy to sort out, however, so I decided to contact him at his place of work. When he came to the phone he was obviously surprised and caught unawares. He was very defensive and seemed very cross that Mduduza had stolen the money. He did not show much compassion for his son, saying that if the boy wanted anything from him he must come to him personally and that he did not have time for at least another week. It was apparent that he did not really care about the child, so I just told him that the boy would give him his money back. At least this would give Mduduza the peace of mind to return to his mother. After talking with Mduduza I decided to go with him and visit his mother. Mduduza was excited. He said he would stay there if I could make a way. I told him that I would do that if his mother was willing.

We set off in the pick-up truck to the little township near Durban International Airport. Mduduza directed me to his mother's house and as we approached it I was somehow relieved to see that his mother lived in a quiet neighbourhood where the local kids played outside in the streets. However, when we got to the door we were greeted by a child quite unfamiliar to Mduduza, who proceeded to tell him that his mother had left and that she did not know where she was now. This was a blow. We were upset. I had bought Mduduza a new set of clothes and toiletries, and

had a plan to support him financially each month. I could
see the disappointment in his face as he bravely tried to hide
it. He looked smart, he wanted to impress his mother, he
was desperate to be received well by her. Mduduza had
thought that he was going home, leaving the streets. He had
not expected this turn of events and so out of desperation he
decided to take us to his father in the township of Inanda.

Mduduza was sure that he knew the way to his father's
house and I followed his intricate directions closely. Before
long we had been right the way through the vast township.
The further we went the more I started to lose hope of
finding his father's house. Eventually the road ran out and
we just stopped and looked at each other. Night was falling
and our hopes had been dashed once again. Again desperate, Mduduza started asking passers-by if they knew his
father. No one did – my heart went out to him. My
emotions were lodged somewhere between extreme frustration after having driven so far with so much hope, and
despair and helplessness as I thought of Mduduza having to
go back to the streets. I couldn't understand how God could
let us go so far, getting so excited, almost getting him off the
streets and yet have nothing to show for it at the end of the
day. It was the old cliché, 'so near but yet so far'.

We returned to the streets. It was hopeless trying to get
Mduduza to a project because of his glue addiction and the
close proximity of the projects to town. This combination
would have made him run away almost instantly, back to
the streets. I promised Mduduza that I would try to contact
his father again. Reluctantly, Mduduza took off his new
'going home' clothes and put on his ragged, filthy street
clothes. He was sniffing harder and harder on his glue
bottle, slowly killing the pain but never really escaping.
I went back to my flat where I watched him from my
window as he sat dejectedly on the streets, high, in a
confused state, trying desperately to come to terms with
his situation. He sat until his eyes closed and he slept. As I

watched him I thought to myself, 'Why does this lad have such a hard life? He doesn't deserve it.'

I pondered this as I retired to my comfortable, warm bed. I could not even give him a bed for the night because I was a single young man on my own. Why had I been so fortunate as to be born into a happy family while he had been so unfortunate and born into poverty?

I had made arrangements to meet with Mduduza at 4 o'clock in the afternoon the next day. When that time came, as I approached the appointed area, I found him lying in a foetal position on the road with his oversized, dirty coat pulled over his head. His friends looked on anxiously and when they spotted me they ran over to me to tell me that Mduduza was hurt.

As I pulled the coat away from Mduduza's face I was shocked to see a big, bloody graze on his forehead, another in the area between his nose and his upper lip, an even bigger one on his shoulder and small ones over his hands. A security guard outside an Irish theme pub in down-town Durban had beaten him up. As he had been walking past a row of parked cars in the streets one of the car guards had stopped him, suspecting him of trying to break into a car. As the car guard proceeded to check the car and the boy he realised that it was a mistake, nothing had been done. The car guard let him go and as the boy started to walk away another security guard came over with a sjambok (a heavy whip) and started beating him. Mduduza jumped and started running but as he did so the security guard tripped him up. Passers-by gasped at the cruelty as they watched the little boy take a beating for no reason, and looked on in horror as the security guard's boot caught the boy's little feet and sent his helplessly unco-ordinated body crashing down face first on to the concrete. A traffic warden had witnessed the attack and started to write down the details. But when he looked more closely at Mduduza he stopped writing, probably thinking, albeit with compassion, 'What's the point? Nothing would be done about this boy. After all, he is just a street child.' Mduduza bawled his eyes out, sucked deeply on his glue and lay huddled on the ground. He got up and hobbled back to his position outside my flat and collapsed, a dishevelled wreck.

It was the last straw. As Mduduza explained to me what had happened, it was as if he was having a breakdown. I took him to the hospital where it was established that there were no broken bones. I then took him to the pharmacy where I bought bandages and antiseptic creams and bandaged him up. I must admit that in a cruel sort of way he looked almost funny in his bandages. He had insisted on having a bandage put underneath his nose on his top lip. As he walked around he looked like something out of the cartoons, an absolute walking disaster.

The next day he got worse emotionally. He was so damaged by glue and once again was acting quite irrationally. However, there was one significant piece of news: he had remembered that there was a relative of his working in town and she would know where his mother stayed. This was great and I arranged with the lady who was in fact his aunt to meet us at the end of the day. When this time arrived Mduduza was so high that, as I removed his bandages to let the wounds breathe, he insisted on being bandaged up again becoming obsessive about this idea. I told him that it would not do any good, at which he became very upset. This time it was a little incident like this that caused him to break down again. With no real reason he decided that he would not come to pick up his aunt.

The time had passed, we had not met up with his aunt, but sure enough as soon as it was too late he changed his mind again. I said to him that fifteen minutes ago we could have gone, but now we would have to wait until tomorrow. Mduduza had totally lost it. He suddenly decided that he wanted to go and sleep in another part of town, saying that he did not want any more help and that I was making a fool out of him. He asked for his bandages and said that he was going. I knew that it was his glue speaking and that he was desperately seeking attention so I played along by saying, 'If you want to go, that's fine but I will be here waiting for you when you need me.'

I then walked away and as I did so he ran after me, sobbing and saying, 'I'm going to kill myself' while miming the action of a knife across his throat.

Enough was enough and I said to him softly, 'Come, let's go for a chat. We'll put your antiseptic cream on at the same time.'

He came and we talked and as we did so it suddenly dawned on me that he had somehow reached rock bottom. He was clutching at anything, his life depended on this. Something spiritually significant was happening at this time. God seemed to give him supernatural strength just as he reached the end of his tether. In the midst of his pathetic state God stepped in. Suddenly Mduduza had a peace about him. As we chatted and I bandaged him up, he started to relax and we made a plan to meet up with his aunt the next day. Relief came over him. I cannot really explain it, but I think that the Holy Spirit was working in him.

The next day went smoothly. I picked up Mduduza and we went to meet his aunt from her work. His aunt was very friendly and directed us straight to his mother's new shack. Mduduza's mother had moved from her small house on one side of the township to a little shack a few kilometres away. The day that we went to his mother it was raining. For- tunately, I was driving the pick-up truck which handled the small mud road to her shack well. We jumped out of the vehicle. Mduduza was excited. I did not know what to expect; would his mother be pleased, cross, disinterested, or maybe after a fast buck at his expense? It was a wonderful experience watching a mother and son reunite. She was sitting on a couch and instantly beckoned him over to sit with her where she cuddled and caressed him. That his mother really loved him was evident as she was so thrilled to see him. She asked me to sit down and told me that she was very grateful to have her son back but she was concerned as to whether he would stay or run away again. I arranged with her that we would support Mduduza for a period of six months, then I would review the situation.

It was so exciting to watch God's plan coming together, one day after the boy had reached rock bottom. In the vehicle I had spoken with Mduduza about how much God loved him and he had listened intently. As we arrived at his mother's shack, a group of local Christians also arrived to have a Bible study with his mother who, it seems, also has a faith. As we all sat there everything seemed so right.

At the time of writing, Mduduza lives happily with his mother. He is still vulnerable to his glue addiction, he could still run back to the streets if things do not go smoothly at home. He still desperately needs our prayers and although this could be perceived as a happy ending and is quite clearly a miracle, Mduduza's struggle will continue as he tries to regain his lost childhood. The damage caused by years of street life may slowly emerge and as he starts to pick up the pieces he will need God's Holy Spirit to comfort and support him. He will also have to work hard to make up for his lost years in education; he has a long road ahead. At fourteen, Mduduza has seen the harsh reality of life; his experiences have been more traumatic than those of most adults. We need to pray now more than ever for his life, for God's continued help. As he battles a long life's road he now has hope, he now has a chance. With hard work he too can achieve some of his dreams, he too can make something of his life. I know that one thing is for sure: God didn't bring him this far to leave him.

10   Dropping in

Throughout my time in South Africa I have been fortunate enough to have had a steady flow of visitors and volunteers – many from the UK – to whom I am indebted not only for their practical help but for their support, encouragement and friendship. These visitors have helped me to observe the work from the outside as they have offered useful advice, as well as quite often helpful criticism. Since the early days of my work, members of my family have come out for short periods of time for working holidays, with more emphasis on the working! Ben was out at a time when donations were desperately needed to clothe the children at Isaiah 58 and he was able to accompany me on the long drive from East London to Durban to pick up the consignment of clothes from the docks, a donation from the UK. Abi, my sister, helped out on a number of occasions and on her first trip she helped out with the Christmas activities at Isaiah 58. She loved it, despite Auntie Maggie's constant attempts to chain her to the kitchen! A few years later she came back and was able to help on a trip with the Daily Bread children to the Addo Elephant Game Park near Port Elizabeth.

Joe, my youngest brother, came out toward the end of 1996 and his trip was very interesting, as he was the same age as many of the children at Isaiah 58. He was a blessing in disguise. On the one hand it was often quite impossible to get him to help out in certain areas. On the other, what I noticed was that perhaps because of being the same age as the older kids he entered the project in a completely different way from most other volunteers. Of course, he was still compassionate to their pasts, but where others have gone in and been totally overcome with emotion at the whole concept of the project he went in with a different approach, one of getting to know a new group of contemporaries and making new friends.

Instead of speaking in ridiculously clear pidgin English and waving arm movements to the children, then saying, 'Ah, what a lovely child,' and patting them on the head, he went in with a more natural, slightly apprehensive yet friendly attitude, getting to know each child before making sweeping statements about how lovely they were. After a while he was chatting away with them about rap music, soccer, basketball, clothes and probably girls! I was just thrilled to have him out in South Africa visiting me. I had not taken into consideration just how valuable his input would be in becoming a real outside friend to the kids.

One close friend of mine had quite an experience in South Africa as he arrived during the election period of 1994 amid rumours of civil war and unrest. Mark Hagley, the owner of plain lazy surf wear, was so intimidated by these wild rumours that it made his trip quite a nerve-wracking experience and he decided to reschedule his trip home. The only problem was that the day of his rescheduled flight was ironically the only day that a bomb went off in South Africa during that period. It happened at Johannesburg Airport so as he flew from East London to Jo'burg he flew into chaos! The rest of South Africa was remarkably peaceful. Thankfully he was safe, that is until the subject was brought up at his wedding.

Each person who visited would try to utilise any skill that they had to offer with the children. Another friend of mine, Kristen Meadows, was able to train the Isaiah 58 children in basketball on a new basketball court. He has long been involved with the sport in the UK. Kris took the working/ holidays idea as literally as possible, sleeping and relaxing each day until about 2 p.m. having watched CNN all morning, after which he would drift into Isaiah 58 and give 110 per cent until late at night!

Occasionally I have dropped my friends in at the deep end. One such occasion was when I embellished a story about a friend of mine who was visiting to help out at Isaiah 58. I told the children that he was coming to be their football coach for a month or two. Fortunately Jeremy Radcliffe can rise to a challenge and together we devised a series of training moves that we had learned by watching the film *Escape to Victory* with Pele, Ossie Ardiles and Sylvester Stalone. I think the team benefited more through the morale boost at this stage than through the coaching, but they certainly became very fond of their new coach.

Another classic example was my good friend, Stephen Bewes, who is an obsessive trumpeter. Steve certainly caused a stir with his shaven bald head, Yul Brynner style, and his shining trumpet. Steve kept crowds entertained wherever he went by picking up two extremely well-known tunes, first '*Nkosi Sikelela iAfrika*', the wonderfully rich South African national anthem and anthem of the struggle, which he played Hugh Masekela style. The second was that of a hugely successful *kwaito* (local) tune by a band called TKZ which drove the young people wild. The people could not believe it when he started playing and the kids at both Daily Bread and Isaiah 58 loved him, nicknaming him 'Peanut' after his hairstyle – or lack of it. Whether it was to a street child on the streets of Durban, the kids at the projects in East London, countless petrol attendants throughout the Transkei or revellers at the beach, Steve was a great source of entertainment and made many friends.

After having so many visitors, mostly friends and family, it became apparent how useful visitors were in helping with the work and through sending back newsletters and information to the UK, quite a few young people were asking about the possibilities of voluntary work with me at the projects. I took on quite a few unofficial short-time workers, all of whom contributed much. I soon decided to bring out an official volunteer. The first person who came out as an official Amos Trust volunteer was a girl called Anna Joseph from Christchurch, Virginia Water in Surrey, England. Anna came to help me at Isaiah 58. She was great, very willing to get stuck in, which was fortunate because the whole set-up was very ad hoc as she was my first real volunteer. It was a period of learning for me and I started to really think of how volunteers could best be utilised in the work. Anna formed strong bonds on the streets with the girls, particularly Felicia and she became a great encouragement to them and the children of Isaiah 58.

The word 'volunteer' can have many connotations. What does the volunteer do? Do they do the dirty work? Do they preach? Do they answer the phones? First, to be able to understand the Amos Trust volunteer thinking we have to look at how overseas Christian workers have been perceived in the past by the communities that they came out to serve. There are two main reasons that volunteers come to South Africa and the first one is that of evangelism. Many Christians still regard Africa as the mission field and to some it is the training ground for mission work. I have watched some missionaries using rural African people as a way of getting used to preaching and standing up in front of people. Sometimes they preach in straight English, pouring out their well-rehearsed testimony, getting louder as they gain confidence. Once they have become more confident they rarely go back to those rural Africans.

Missionaries to Africa have not always portrayed the true heart of Christianity and have often frowned upon local culture instead trying to convert people to their own culture. This has had a damaging effect in its paternalism, especially as Jesus taught the way of humble friendships, the quiet revolution and the concepts of mutual respect and equality. Missionaries have been seen to stand for control, the destruction of African cultures, paternalism and inequality.

We must change the belief that we as Westerners have the 'God-given' lifestyle to which other cultures should conform, because we have systematically damaged most parts of the world. Indeed Britain and the West have polluted the rest of the world with such evils as extreme capitalism, alcoholism, sexual immorality, guns and other things.

'I'm on the mission to save people' thinking can often lead to frenzied 'saving' sprees. The up side is that perhaps this gives people the opportunity to consider Jesus Christ, but at the end of the day these whirlwind evangelists leave a trail of confusion. People are thought of as numbers and little thought is given to how Christ is applicable in their own culture. Quite often the preacher hasn't got a clue about the culture that they are preaching in.

I do believe in spreading the word of Jesus Christ, the Saviour of all, but I also feel that we should think long term about how we portray the life of Christ. After all, to the non-believer the way of Christ is portrayed in his followers. Although Christianity is practised widely in black South Africa, it is often seen as the white man's religion that brought with it apartheid and all its horrors. Indeed, the Church quite often supported apartheid in as much as many denominations did not take a stand against the system. Many Christians supported apartheid. This is far removed from the reality of the all-inclusive love of God that is at the heart of the Christian faith and is not, I imagine, quite what Jesus had in mind when he said, 'Go to all the ends of the earth and spread the good news.' The key phrase here is that he said it was 'good news' and it was for everybody. When people are oppressed in the name of Christianity it is quite honestly 'bad news' for the community on the receiving end, so one must start asking questions as to the validity of the theology of their oppressors.

The second main reason for people to have worked as volunteers in South Africa is to try to help make a difference socially. A few of these people have found it really hard to shake off the Western feeling of superiority, making rash judgments and premature decisions, but there is a core of the more humble types who have come out with one intention: to serve. Praise God for the servants, those who simply want to serve in whatever way their skills enable them. Praise him for the servers who are willing to do it the local way and those who don't arrive with the answers but with an open heart. Praise him for those committed to listening and then fighting for the dignity of the community, for those committed to learning about their traditions, tasting their foods, learning their languages, going to their churches and fellowshipping their way. Then when they have earned the right to, they can share their own experiences and culture in a passive but open way, recognising their own strengths and weaknesses.

So the key word here is to *serve*. The concept of going as a volunteer worker in a foreign land in the area of social justice has, for effectiveness and ethical reasons, to be one of going to serve the local community. I believe it is ethically corrupt to operate outside the local community, which is why it is vital to have local support and direction.

The white churches in South Africa have a real responsibility in as much as they are often the churches with money; therefore they are able to communicate internationally, making contact with potential visitors to the country. All too often, groups of Christians from the UK and other countries come out to South Africa on outreach tours and are just kept within the white communities, with a possible exception of a quick trip into one of the townships to say that they have been into a township. The problem here is not necessarily that of the visitors, although they too have a responsibility to think about the social situation of any country that they visit. These people do not end up seeing the real South Africa and often come back with a warped perception of life in the country. I believe it is the responsibility of the white churches to share such visitors with black churches. In many cases, UK visitors that I have met have expressed their frustration at not being able to see the real South Africa. They would dearly love to be able to stay with a black family and to sacrifice the endless swimming pools and barbecues that they had to endure. At the end of the day, both the visitors and the black churches are being robbed of potential encouragement and fellowship through listening and sharing.

We specifically want Amos Trust volunteers to come to South Africa to serve the street children. When on the streets they might be directly serving the street children amid a local team. However, when working in a project like Isaiah 58 or Daily Bread they will serve those workers who are already serving the street children and who will continue to serve them once the volunteers are gone.

After Anna Joseph's visit, I realised how helpful volunteers are, especially as they are usually so dedicated and willing to get their hands dirty. The Amos Trust were able to facilitate more volunteers and in 1996 an 18-year-old lad called Joe Walker came out to be an Amos Trust volunteer working with me at the Isaiah 58 project. This was his first trip to South Africa, and his job was to help with the recreational development of the children, spending almost his entire day from seven o'clock in the morning to about nine o'clock at night at the project. He would play with the kids, help on outings, encourage Auntie Maggie, and sing and help in the evening prayer time. He absolutely fell in love with the work. One thing I noticed about Joe was that there was a unique streak in him. As well as loving the work at the homes, he was becoming particularly dedicated to the street work and would come with me every night to work with those kids still on the streets. He saw some quite heavy sights that most 18-year-olds in the UK would never see. He also earned the trust of the toughest street kids.

At the age of twenty in 1998 Joe came back again for

three months. This time it was slightly different. It was not his first time, he had learned the ropes, he knew what to do. It was just a case of getting down to it. Joe was now able to focus particularly on the streets, covering a lot of ground in the process. He spent a lot of time chatting with and serving the Point Road street children in Durban and the links that he made were really valuable to my work. He started an evening soccer routine where all the local street kids would turn up for a soccer match, some food and a good old chinwag. He did a lot of groundwork which is the key to any street children work, and he personally heard the children's stories as he tirelessly combed the streets. I had to laugh. He was so dedicated to street work that I would have to force him to take a rest but he would just say that he was going to the shops or to the beach and I knew full well that he was going back on to the streets to check up on the children.

I sent Joe to various different projects to observe for short periods of time – including a Youth for Christ project in Petermaritzburg, the Miracle House in Aliwal North and Daily Bread in East London – and after each one he would prepare a report that was really helpful to me as well as a way for him to remember his experiences. He also rekindled his links with the children of Isaiah 58 who were thrilled to see him return to South Africa. Joe has now spent much time with the street kids and in the various different projects, and this has had an amazing effect on him, so much so that he feels that vocationally he may be called to work with street children. However, it was not all easy. Miracle House was the hardest and most challenging experience of his life. Durban street work was exciting, challenging in its own way. There were times when Joe felt like crying during his trip to South Africa, due to his emotional and physical experiences, and yet there were times of pure elation as he mingled with the children and was really able to see development in their lives. I think that this is a fair representation of the work.

Before returning to the UK, Joe also spent time with community worker Patrick Lottering, where he lived in the local township, learning about the local culture, politics and South Africa in general. Pat and his wife Hayley looked after Joe very well, as they have done with many of my visitors, spoiling him rotten, spending time with him and feeding him very generously.

In contrast to Joe's street work, but equally as successful, was the Amos Volunteer Team of 1997 which consisted of four young people from the UK who came out to work specifically at the project Daily Bread in East London. The team came from very different backgrounds and consisted of two women in their early to mid-twenties from Camberwell, south London, Tracey Campbell and Jeanette Barrett, one 18-year-old lad from St Saviour's church in Guildford, Patrick Gillespie, and a long-time friend of mine from Portsmouth, Anna Jones.

The team was unique in its visual make-up with Tracey and Jeanette being black and Anna and Patrick being white. It was the first mixed-race volunteer team that I have ever seen in South Africa. As a team we certainly caused a stir. As we went around, people would say 'Hey, look! It's the rainbow nation!' The kids at Daily Bread loved the team, whose specific brief was to serve the local team at the project.

On arrival in South Africa the volunteers did not know what to expect. I had told them, quite ridiculously in hindsight, that it was always hot so don't bother bringing a coat. As you may imagine, they arrived on the coldest, wettest day of the year and continued to remind me of my bad advice for the entire duration of their stay!

The sights of the squatter camps shocked the team. They had expected to see poverty but seeing it so close at hand emphasised the reality of the situation. Getting used to the left-overs of the apartheid attitudes was also difficult for the team, and there were many times when they were quietly seething at what they saw. The community received the four volunteers very well. As was usual Pat and Hayley rallied round to help them and introduced them to other members of the community.

Being a volunteer group can be tough. Your personal space is often encroached upon but it teaches you team-work. The six-month period that these particular volunteers came out for had its ups and downs; however, the emphasis was on the ups. All four volunteers were instrumental in some major developments in the lives of the children too. Occasionally the volunteers would fight with each other but that was OK, it was all part of the learning experience. One of my favourite stories is that of when Tracey and Patrick had a little fall-out in the supermarket. I was not there but I wish I had been just for the pure entertainment. Even in post-election South Africa, the sight of a group of black-and-white young people walking together, buying food collectively in the supermarket causes a stir. However, a full-on argument between a black girl and a white boy about what food to buy was the greatest value-for-money entertainment. The other shoppers must have looked on in amazement as they hurled insults at each other. The fight was short-lived and one of the many stages of team development.

Almost all the children at Daily Bread will agree that the volunteers' time with them was not only a time of social liberation and a time of joy but also one of spiritual liberation and identity-searching. Patrick had the toughest job. He was assigned to the older boys' farm where he embarked on the near-impossible task of taking on the recreational activities of the boys. Against all odds he got stuck in and achieved much, forming good friendships with the children. He worked alongside Mike Nomtoto and particularly helped with soccer, table tennis and beach trips. He was able to chat with and become very close to the boys, many of whom were the same age as him, a few were even older. He became a mate to them and with creativity was able to get involved with the activities, never patronising them or assuming that he had all the answers. He worked very closely with another UK volunteer called Mark who had not come out through the Amos Trust but had specifically come to help the government school on site. Mark and Patrick became very good friends and both got involved recreationally at the farms, focusing particularly on drama and even putting on a spectacular performance of *Julius Caesar* at Daily Bread. The kids loved it. Patrick also became involved with the recreational activities of the small boys as well – I'm sure he needed a big holiday once he had finished.

The volunteers made clear from the beginning that they were Christians, much to the delight of the housemother Nosimo who was herself a committed Christian. I remember their first day at the projects. The girls all gathered when the female volunteers arrived. There was much excitement and singing from Daily Bread girls, who then asked each of the new volunteers to sing a song! Fortunately for us at least Tracey and Jeanette were both musically inclined so they saved us embarrassment. Tracey 'rapped', to the sheer excitement of the girls, and Jeanette sang. Anna and myself were slightly less forthcoming. Fortunately I knew all the girls so in the end I sang a song. No, I'm not saying which one! Anna and I got off lightly.

The girls at Daily Bread did not have much daily activity. They had come from some horrific backgrounds and were really hungry for any type of input, whether it be spiritual or social. Each child was searching for real love, real friendships, real shoulders to cry on, people who cared on a personal level. They did, of course, have Nosimo and the other housemothers who gave so much of their time for such small rewards, and to whom the girls were very closely attached; yet they too needed support.

Possibly the most important way that the team met

people from the local community was through becoming part of a local church. In the past the children had periodically visited local churches in East London but had never really become seriously involved in a church family. I had started to take the children to a local charismatic church in East London because they translated their service into Xhosa. However, the girls complained that the people at the church kept trying to make them fall over when they came up for prayer and saying that they applied force to their foreheads to make them 'go down'.

God had a master plan up his sleeve. Acting on an invitation of a friend the female volunteers took the girls to a church in a nearby black township called Zwelitsha. The church was called the 'Divine Life Centre' and was a black Pentecostal church – South African style – with a heavy emphasis on gospel music. Two of the best gospel choirs in South Africa come from within the congregation. Both of these had released CDs and had much local and national support. One thing that was guaranteed at their services was good worship times and when I say 'good' I mean 'wonderful'. At times I caught myself thinking, 'This is it, this is what heaven will sound like.' Apart from the outstanding musical quality in the church the congregation were the most open, welcoming and downright friendly group of people I had ever come across. The children were welcomed with open arms, not in a patronising way but with that of mutual respect. The kids were thrilled. The volunteers became celebrities after Tracey 'rapped' in church, and the congregation embarked on strengthening the links they had with the girls of Daily Bread by visiting the projects and having services at the girls' farm. The church was predominantly made up of young people with a few wise elders to support, and this perhaps accounted for the unusual vibrancy of the congregation. They had become committed to their relationship with Daily Bread and often held services at the project as well as inviting the girls to their church camp, paying all their expenses. The children were so excited about this gospel of Jesus that had revived a hope and given them friends and a family.

Early on in their stay, the volunteers started a voluntary Bible study for the girls. At first it took place twice a week in the evenings but soon it became so over-subscribed by the girls that it became a daily Bible study. The children used it as a time to cry out to God for help without any inhibition. Sometimes the girls would cry uncontrollably as God's comforting Spirit ministered to them. At other times they would listen attentively as the volunteers or Nosimo would preach from the Bible in Xhosa. Obviously the volunteers would use a translator. I would often turn up late in the evening after a hard day at the boys' farm and simply sit under the palm tree outside, listening to the girls singing, knowing that God was at work with his healing way of peace and love. As I mentioned earlier, Tracey and Jeanette were very musically inclined. Tracey was a member of a gospel choir at her church in Camberwell and Jeanette was the worship leader at the same church. After hearing the quality of the Daily Bread girls' singing and seeing the other choirs at the church, they decided to start to train the girls to sing together as a choir. It was then that the Nu Hope gospel choir was formed and after practising very hard for some time they were ready to perform.

The girls at the farm were so excited by all the changes that they decided among themselves to put on a thanksgiving concert to say thanks for all the new innovations and to introduce themselves to the church as the Nu Hope gospel choir. It was a marvellous day with a huge turn-out in the school building at Daily Bread. The other gospel choirs from the church performed first, with the grand finale being performed by the Nu Hope choir. The crowd went wild. The applause was huge. The girls had given an outstanding performance and received a standing ovation. They were now a force to be reckoned with on the gospel scene! Tracey and Jeanette continued to train them throughout the following months and the girls soon became seasoned performers.

The spiritual aspect of the volunteers' work was by no means the only aspect of what they did. Along with it came endless hours of practical, physical serving of the project as drivers, cleaners, cooks, sports coaches, activity co-ordinators and a whole host of other things. Each school holidays they would plan an activities programme for the children. Anna is a very capable sports person and used to be involved with a volleyball team herself. She was able to use these skills and taught the girls volleyball and organised sports days which the girls loved. The girls played some netball matches against the children of Isaiah 58. I had to remain neutral in my support between Isaiah 58 and Daily Bread, but the Isaiah girls had not had much netball coaching so it was a walk-over for the Daily Bread girls.

Volunteers' achievements should not be measured solely in terms of the time that they are at the project but also on the sustainability of their inputs after they have gone. It was vital for the team to work closely with and take direction from such people as Nosimo and Mike who were only too ready to train the volunteers and to utilise their ideas and support.

If I could sum up the impact of the four volunteers over six months, I would say that as well as serving the project and children they encouraged them to the extent of giving them new hope. The Amos volunteers have all walked into situations very different to their home environments, far removed from their comfort zones, yet in all cases have come back with changed perspectives on life. Jeanette reminisced recently on the phone to me, saying, 'When I announced I was off to South Africa to serve the street children, people back home called me crazy for going. However, when I got back I realised that I would have been crazy for not going!'

Jeanette went on to conclude that linking arms with such dedicated South Africans and serving a wonderful group of children made her realise that no matter how insignificantly we view ourselves we all have the capacity to serve, encourage and make a difference.

As we progress through the turn of the millennium, I hope to be able to facilitate more Amos volunteers as well as local volunteers to help with my street work in Durban as well as to serve the shelters and children's homes.

11   The gift

In six and a half years of working on the streets of East
London and Durban, there have been many faces that have
come and gone. Kids have ventured on to the streets but
gone home at the end of the day. Others keep on returning,
some go to the projects, and some never leave the streets.
One thing that all these children have in common is that at
least at one stage in their short lives they have felt real
suffering whether it be through poverty, illness, abuse or a
mixture of these. Sometimes the transition into new life can
be painful. One girl has had a major impact on my life in
South Africa and her rescuing has through no fault of her
own been an ongoing struggle. This girl has suffered so
much rejection yet has remained optimistic, desperately
searching for her peace even in the face of some of the
worst horrors of the streets.

I first met Siphokazi around 1995 when I was living in a
ground-floor flat on the beachfront in East London. One
night three street children came and asked me if they could
sleep on my porch to escape from the cold wind and rain.
I knew that my landlord would have had a fit if he knew
that I was allowing street children to sleep on his property.
I decided to allow them to sleep there for one night as it was
late, but only if they agreed to discuss the possibility of
going to one of the projects the following day. I vaguely
remember Siphokazi being one of those children, and it was
she who reminded me of this incident. The next morning
when I awoke, the kids were gone. I thought that I would
catch up with them later on the streets.

However, for a while I did not see or hear from

Siphokazi. I did not know this but she had actually gone to one of the projects, a certain initiative which is no longer running for street children. This would be one of her many attempts to seek refuge from life on the streets.

Siphokazi and her identical twin sister had been living in the Transkei. They lived in a poor area but they were safe; that is, until their mother and father separated. Siphokazi does not know why they separated but remembers her father warning them all to leave the area and also warning her that if she ever used his surname he would kill her. This massive rejection saw her mother take the two children to East London where they moved between friends' shacks, never finding their own place to stay. Her mother became an alcoholic and lost the ability to look after the children who began wandering around the township. Siphokazi's sister was taken in by an aunt, but she had the means only to look after one of the girls so Siphokazi was left with no safe place to live. Siphokazi took to the streets in desperation to survive.

In early 1996 she arrived at Isaiah 58 late one night with two other small children. She could not stay at Isaiah 58 at the time as it was at full capacity and I was having difficulty keeping the doors open for new children. I realised that she had come straight from the other project where she had been staying. I tried to negotiate with her to go back to the other project and she left the next morning to return there, or so I thought. I found out only later that she had allegedly been raped by the worker in charge of this supposed safe place that she had sought refuge at. She was running now from this. At the time she did not tell us this. The account of the event remains unchanged in 1998, nearly three years later. The alleged rapist had led her into nearby bushes where he said they would look for a 'shack' belonging to some street children, to rescue them from the streets. But when they came to the small clearing he told her to take off her clothes so that they could inspect whether she was too old to stay in the children's facility. Confused and scared, she did as she was told because she didn't want to go back to the streets. He climbed on top of her and raped her. Back at the project, she told the man's wife. The wife cried and then together with her husband decided to send Siphokazi back to the streets. She was twelve at the time, just starting to go through puberty. Siphokazi did return to the streets as did two other girls the same man tried to sexually assault one night when his wife was away, but fortunately he was less successful on those occasions. As in the case of most children in this situation, there was just nobody trusted to tell her story to at the time and so Siphokazi lived in silence alone with her secret. If only we had known the real reason she was running.

So Siphokazi landed right back on the streets, after her second attempt to find safety at Isaiah 58, and once again sank straight back into street life. She returned to that which was most familiar to her – the East London streets where she continued to struggle to survive. Her favourite haunt was outside a video arcade on the beachfront where she would beg from passers-by for loose change. Soon her familiarity to that area made her a target for local paedophiles, who started using her regularly as a prostitute, paying her about one pound a time or less depending on the job. She had so little self-love and no guidance on the streets; she was hungry and desperate to survive.

Her abusers were mostly white men living in the Quigney area of East London. In many cases we knew who these people were and where they lived but it was so difficult to do anything about them legally. Another man who lived at the back of a block of flats told her that he and his wife would look after her; however, his wife was away at the time. She stayed there for one night but insisted on separate beds. The man became furious and threw her back out on to the streets, perpetuating the cycle of rejection and behaviour that told her that all she was good for was having sex. Not only was she caught up in a web of prostitution but she was also a target for rape on the streets. In her early years she had used her tomboy looks to disguise herself as a boy but it was becoming almost impossible as her body began to develop, displaying the young woman within her. At around this time I started noticing her on the streets and began chatting to her. I was amazed by her fluency in English. She said she had learnt it as a small child playing with the white children at her mother's place of work.

One of the things that struck me was that although her life was a story of poverty and affliction she was at the same time helping someone who she considered to be worse off than herself. At the age of thirteen, Siphokazi had taken a 9-year-old boy called Vuyo under her wing and through her prostitution was providing for both of them. They would sleep innocently together in different locations. She became like a mother or sister to him. Vuyo was a scared little boy who had been sexually abused by men in the Quigney area of East London.

Vuyo used to wait for me outside the gym that I swam at and we would chat. I was trying to build up a relationship with him that would eventually allow him to trust me enough to take him off the streets. One evening I met with him and asked him if he wanted to get off the streets. He decided that he was ready and I took him down to Isaiah 58. Isaiah 58 was full at the time but I bent the rules because he was so young. Vuyo ran away three times but every time he ran to an area where he knew that I would find him. The last time that he did it I sat him down in the office, shouted at him in disciplining him, and told him it was his last chance. He never ran away again and lives happily at Isaiah 58 to this day.

Many things amazed me about Siphokazi. She was extremely compassionate to others, loved children and animals, was highly intellectual although not educated to a high standard, and was also blessed with a wonderful sense of humour. Despite her hard life she remained one of the most optimistic girls that I had ever known on the streets.

I became desperate. I could not bear to see Siphokazi on the streets. I was determined to find a place for her to live. The projects in East London were not admitting children at that stage so I endeavoured to try to find a Christian family for her to live with. Unfortunately, families willing to take on street kids are few and far between. One family agreed to have her for a month and after that another family took her indefinitely. They really tried hard but they decided to say 'no' after a few weeks, not because they disliked her but because they were worried about the practicalities such as the AIDS issue. They were especially fearful of their children playing with her each day and becoming attached to her. After a while a black social worker said she would take her in, which we were thrilled about. At this stage I was out of the country for a few months. When I returned I heard that the social worker had sent her up to a place called Alice to be with her mother. Siphokazi was unhappy, complaining of being treated like a maid. And so Siphokazi ran away once again. Back on the streets, she found that I was not around and sadly slid back into the old life again, which is so easy to do. Again she appeared destined for street life.

An Amos Trust volunteer called Ellie and I had encouraged Siphokazi to develop a personal relationship with God. She had learnt, through the unstable period of moving around before being placed with the social worker, to really trust God, pray to him and to study children's Bible supplements. It may have been her faith that saved her because while she was on the streets a woman called Miranda befriended her. She took pity on her and used to help her regularly. After a while she arranged for Siphokazi to stay with her sister in a village near Umtata.

Siphokazi stayed happily with Miranda's sister, Mrs Bambeni, for a few months until one day when she was sent to the shops with some money to buy groceries, as was usual. Siphokazi made a bad choice and spent some of the money on herself. From her past experiences of people, she automatically assumed that the woman would no longer welcome her at her house. She stayed on the streets in Umtata, afraid to go home. Ironically, Mrs Bambeni was worried sick about her.

This time she ran to the local streets where she involved herself in prostitution. She worked as a prostitute alongside a group of older women in Umtata. She used to wait on a certain street with the other girls, and men would pull up in expensive cars and take their pick. Often the men would request the youngest girl so she would inevitably be selected. The men who were predominantly white would not usually beat her but she remembers one man in particular who allegedly owns a pharmacy in Umtata. She said that this man did not even wear a condom. She was raped twice and decided she was safer back on the East London streets so she caught a taxi back.

On arrival in East London she met the same familiar faces on the streets. One of the boys who had just got out of prison, Phumlani, told Siphokazi that I was back in town. She came looking for me and found me at the Daily Bread offices. I was thrilled to see her but devastated that she was back in the streets. She finally told me the whole story of the previous six months, which was painful and difficult for me to hear. She told me how she still trusted in God and knew that he would help her, and as she said this to me I couldn't help but wonder why a heart so willing to trust had to endure so much suffering. We were back to square one. I did not have anywhere for her to go and she was now fourteen. The projects were full again and I thought and prayed to God for an answer, for someone to look after her. She had not told me yet about the Umtata incident with the money issue and being afraid of going back. The Daily Bread fund-raiser, Michelle Wileman, a woman committed to children, offered to take her in temporarily until we found a place for her. Siphokazi became very good friends with Michelle's daughter but it was unfair to expect Michelle to continue looking after her as she was a single parent herself. I still could not find a long-term secure place for her. After a while Michelle secured her a place at another children's home, again very temporarily, for only a week.

In desperation I told Siphokazi that we were going to have to go back to Umtata to try again there. Siphokazi then told me the whole story of the mistake that she had made. I could not believe it. I said to her 'Why did you not tell me?' I arranged to go back with her to Umtata to explain the situation. We then contacted Miranda who contacted her sister, and everything was sorted out.

Unfortunately I was unable to go to Umtata on the date that was given so my close friend Mike Nomtoto, manager at the boys' farm at the Daily Bread project and church pastor, went in my place. Siphokazi was thrilled. At last she was reunited with the family that wanted to look after her and indeed loved her. Of course they forgave her. Siphokazi even had a little brother in the family, Mr and Mrs Bambeni's 10-year-old son. We all gave thanks to God as once again Siphokazi saw how God had not given up on her.

Mike, Michelle and myself breathed a sigh of relief. She was safe now and loved which was an answer to much prayer. We had all become very fond of her and were deeply concerned about her and finally she had what we most wanted for her, a family.

A happy ending? Not yet! Just one month later Mike received a phone call from Miranda to say that Mrs Bambeni had taken Siphokazi to the doctor and found out that she was pregnant. She had become suspicious after Siphokazi's breasts had changed shape. What a blow! Again, we could not believe it and cried out, 'Why, God?' Somewhere amidst all the prostitution and the rape she had fallen pregnant and it was impossible to say exactly who the father was, although when the child was born it was obvious that he had been a black man. Mrs Bambeni could not afford to look after another child as her husband was not working, and she was panicking. If I could find a way to support the child they could look after it, for this is what they most wanted to do. Siphokazi did not want to abort the child and I supported her fully in this decision to save the child's life. I do not agree with abortion. After much discussion with Siphokazi, allowing her to be part of the decision-making, I realised that we were both wanting the same thing: the child must live. Fortunately with Amos Trust and their resources we were able to take on the responsibility of financially supporting Siphokazi and her baby every month to enable them to continue living with a healthy family.

In May 1998 Siphokazi, whose name means 'a gift', gave birth to a healthy little boy whom she named Siphiwo, also meaning 'gift'. I had had great long chats with Siphokazi about how the child did not represent the evil acts that she had had to endure in the past but was rather a wonderful gift that God had given to her to turn her brokenness into a situation of hope. She holds on to this and continues to trust in God.

Today Siphiwo is a healthy little boy, six months old, and his mother continues to live in peace with the Bambeni family at their home in Umtata. This story is a dramatic miracle and a story of hope, a real-life situation where God has taken a child who has been suffering at the hands of the streets and changed her life completely, giving hope through his never-ending love. Jesus does that though, doesn't he? He changes people's lives. Siphokazi showed a simple yet great faith the entire time that she was on the streets and her faith set her free. Should we be surprised? I am not so sure because the Bible is very clear in James 2: 5: 'Has not God chosen those who are poor in the eyes of the world to be rich in faith and to inherit the kingdom he promised those who love him?'

Siphokazi has been what her name means to me, a gift. She has been my friend and my teacher, allowing me to discover through her faith a God who sees and responds to our cry for help. She has made my life rich, allowing me to pass on the wealth she has given as I serve other kids who are also longing for hope and promise. And this is what we seek for all the children we serve: that they too will grow to discover that their lives are a gift.

12   The missing link

There are many shelters, children's homes and facilities caring for street children in South Africa. There are many dedicated people trying to run these projects as well as a few chancers with dubious aims. Occasionally starting a project for street children is seen as a way of creating an income for oneself with the attraction of being able to fund-raise. Unless completely crooked, people who try this are usually disappointed. Some projects are government-subsidised while most like Miracle House in Aliwal North struggle to make ends meet with little or no support.

There are many successful projects in South Africa but equally as many that simply exist on the borderline, never really achieving their full potential. This is partly to do with difficulty in raising funds and partly to do with the fact that there are no real hard and fast rules about running street children projects and certainly not enough sharing of ideas with other organisations and interested parties. Projects run for the most part as their own little entities and not as part of a larger, more powerful, organised body.

The government is in a slight dilemma because on the one hand they desperately need the support of non-governmental organisations (NGOs) as they do not have the experience, creativity and means to solve many of their welfare problems on their own. But they do not have money to splash out in support of these organisations, which makes the issue of non-duplication paramount as a way of conserving money. Duplication in this context means two or more projects doing the same work in one town. The government tries to avoid registering a project if its work is already done somewhere else. The downside of this situation is that it leaves incredible pressure and responsibility on those organisations that do become subsidised to tackle the problem efficiently for, in a sense, they are the only hope for street children in a particular area. I believe that this problem is particularly far-reaching as it demands the projects to think about every aspect of the work and to ultimately be successful.

In Durban, a street children's forum has been formed to try and bring the organisations together to deal with the street children problem in the area. This is certainly a positive move. If the forum can serve and support the projects that work with the street children while encouraging these projects to work together on the issue it may have a significant impact. Durban needs to face the problem of street children openly and humanely so that in the future when there are major events in town – such as the rugby World Cup, the non-aligned movements summit (NAM) and the Queen's visit – the street children do not simply get rounded up and dumped in shelters or, worse still, in remote distant areas. During the NAM summit the children told a local newspaper reporter of how they had been rounded up and dumped out of town. I spoke with children who said that they had been beaten in the process. Local people have told me of a man (who will remain nameless) who owns a security company in Durban and rounds the children up forcefully and takes them and dumps them far away from Durban. This man was reported to have been asked by an organisation concerned with beachfront business to do this. He had told them that he was going to take them to a shelter, but this was not true. When the Queen came on an official visit to Durban, it is alleged that the children were rounded up and locked up for the duration of her visit. I do not believe that the future of dealing with problems like that of street children is to cover them up by sweeping them under the carpet or hiding them when visitors come to town.

More support may actually come locally and from overseas to help with the problem if the city is honest about the situation. I think the reasons that the police rounded these children up were the fear that a foreign visitor may get mugged and that street children are unsightly and do not leave a good impression. However, although we know that street children can be dangerous, it is unfair to assume that they are responsible for all crime.

A classic example is that of a German tourist murdered on Durban's beachfront one New Year's Eve. The police claimed that he had been murdered by street children and this even hit the international media. I remember being told of the incident by people in England and it was also a prominent national news item. However, after talking to people in Durban I realised that they had actually caught the murderer who was not a street child at all and had no relation to street children. It appeared that perhaps people had needed someone to blame. The story was never corrected in the international media and not much effort was made nationally to inform the public that in fact it had had nothing to do with the street children. The damage was done.

I have mentioned before that working together with the community is the key to finding solutions to these problems and any ideas that I may have to offer would have to be carefully scrutinised and often reshaped by others if they were to be used in finding a solution. I have a structure emerging in my mind that may, however simple, be a starting point to providing the missing links to working with street kids and may in part be applicable and thought-provoking to those people already involved in projects. This structure has emerged through my working on the streets for the last seven years from within children's shelters and homes.

It is a holistic structure, looking at the concept of following through the work from the date of the initial contact with the child on the streets to the day they finally leave the project. You have probably gathered that one of my gripes is that not enough emphasis or importance is put on street work, sometimes referred to as 'outreach'. Indeed most projects simply have an open door policy that says, if the children wander in, we will take them. I believe more in intervention at street level. The open door policy is not sufficient. People need to go to the streets, to the children. This is where I think the missing link lies. I think that street-based projects are needed that identify street children, build relationships with them and then encourage them off the streets either to be reintegrated with their families or, if this is not possible, to be placed in the shelters or homes. This street-based initiative or street team is, I believe, a vital component of the work. Most shelters simply do not have the resources or the time to actively comb the streets and the idea of a street team that serves the homes and shelters with the sole purpose of outreach work could hold the key to the future.

The partnership of street work and residential homes may lead to long-lasting development and to the eventual break-down of street culture. Of course the breakdown of street culture needs to run in partnership with township social programmes dealing with the basic issues that force the children out on to the streets in the first place. The backlog of dealing with the township problems has meant that the 'emergency service' – in other words, the organisations dealing with street children – has been swamped. I believe that in many areas the residential project work is far more advanced than street work and therefore incomplete or at least lopsided in its overall effect on the street child community.

In most cities in South Africa you'll find that many of the street children have been to a project and have run away again. I don't think the problem lies necessarily with the residential care itself as I actually feel that it is not surprising that a child cannot immediately handle the transition from lawless street life to an organised project. No matter how fantastic the project is, a child is going to be intimidated on entry; especially taking into consideration the amount of emotional, psychological and physical baggage that almost all of the children carry with them even before they arrive in the streets. However, if a team works actively on the streets, they may then get to the root of why the children have run away and choose to remain on the streets. They may then begin to understand just exactly what the children have experienced on the streets and how best to deal with that.

It is in Durban that I have started to put this idea into practice by setting up a street team. There are, as I have said, some very good shelters and children's homes in Durban, and what we have done is to bring some of these shelters together to form a managing body to own collectively and oversee a street team to work alongside the street children in the city. The initial role players alongside myself and the Amos Trust have been Youth for Christ, Durban, who run a superb girls' shelter; Streetwise, a shelter for boys; Siyakhiwa boys' shelter; and Sinethemba children's home. They are all good projects, run by dedicated staff hungry for a new approach to street work.

These staff are very under-supported and under a lot of outside pressure to perform but remain committed to the children. Outsiders have in the past called for new 'super' residential projects to be set up to take over from these shelters, but have failed to realise that supporting the existing projects and recognising their hard work would make a big difference. These projects, with financial support and the support of a street team, can revolutionise the situation. It is time for business, the welfare department, the police and the community to listen and respect the ground-level workers who have given endless time devoting themselves to street children.

Each of the projects has made available staff members and social workers to be part of the street team and we have opened up an office on the corner of Point Road and West Street in down-town Durban. This office is a nerve centre of information about the streets and a place where the team can be guided and receive training.

As a new street team in Durban, we have become a recognisable presence on the streets. As a team we comb the streets, chatting with the kids, earning their trust and becoming familiar with the real world of street life. This enables us to start dealing with all aspects of this lifestyle. In the first two months of operating we reunited about ten children with their families. Some of these children come from as far afield as the Orange Free State, the border of Swaziland and the Transkei. These children had run to the big city of Durban in the hope of finding a better life. Some of these children have needed a small amount of temporary financial support to get them integrated into their families.

We have also taken many children to the local shelters. The fact that staff members from these shelters make up the street team has meant that the children have already built relationships with the staff members while on the streets, making the move much easier. As the work on the streets and in the home becomes intertwined it allows us to clearly identify children on the streets who have absconded from projects and then to work through the problems and anxieties that caused them to run away.

At the moment the full street team operates on Mondays, Wednesdays and Fridays, allowing the other days for the team members to be back in their home projects, encouraging those children who have now left the streets. As the team grows, different members will work on the days in between, increasing the presence on the streets.

Tackling the hard issues of street life is an effort to try and break the whole phenomenon down into manageable parts. Girls are particularly vulnerable on the streets and for them life is based on surviving by using the only recognised commodity that they have – their bodies. Although some street girls still beg on the streets, the fact is that they learn to use sex from a very early age to support themselves and also to keep their place in the street groups by satisfying the street boys. Their sexuality is not apparent to them as a gift from God, only as something that they can use to survive. In Durban there are a few street girls actually living on the streets. The high levels of prostitution in the area mean that these girls quickly get caught up in the 'flats' lifestyle. They live in low-cost accommodation, using it as a base for prostitution which not only pays the rent but gives them money to pay for their everyday needs like clothes and toiletries. They soon learn how to keep themselves clean and tidy to attract customers and therefore are very hard to actually identify. Some of the girls may be as young as twelve or thirteen and work as prostitutes. Durban's child prostitutes often serve the sailors visiting from many foreign countries as well as all the communities within the city. Some escort agencies take these young girls and actually give them accommodation together close to the agency itself. Often their clients are looking for the youngest girl available, according to a 15-year-old former child prostitute, who also remarked that these men treat them 'well' and 'don't hurt them'.

This same girl, when talking on the subject of a rape that had happened to her recently remarked, 'It wasn't a very bad rape. He just forced me to have sex. He didn't beat me up.' It is as if these children have come to expect rape so much that they are just thankful when it is not violent. Something is very wrong here.

Our team has embarked on coming to grips with the realities of child prostitution and the 'flats' lifestyle. We have started to identify the girls involved and those at risk and to recognise the dynamics of how these girls work, identifying trouble spots and abusers. I hope we will be able significantly to start attacking the whole evil system of child prostitution.

We have seen in Chapter 4 how vulnerable the girls and boys of the streets are to AIDS. One organisation that had tested about fifteen children told me that eleven of them were HIV-positive. Our street team is going to have to be very much in the front line in the battle against AIDS. It would be very useful to have a team equipped to counsel those children wanting to be tested and those who test positive. We need to spread AIDS awareness on the streets, perhaps putting on creative workshops for the children on the streets and in the projects, to teach them about safe sex. There is so much that can be done to educate the children on how to protect themselves from AIDS. The social workers will be part and parcel of AIDS work within the team.

The problem of glue sniffing is one that the team is addressing. The devastating effect of the glue on the children and the addiction that goes with it are major reasons for kids not settling in the projects. There are certain shop owners known to us who are actually making money off the street kids by selling glue bottles to them for four rand (40p) a bottle. There is one guy who actually drives round locating the children to sell to them. It baffles me as to how he is able to make money out of this. We hope to be able to launch a campaign against such businessmen.

One important job of the street team is to try to identify the potential street children of tomorrow and to work with them to reduce the chances of them living on the streets. Many of these are girls who live with their mothers who beg on the streets. We have started to build very strong links with these mothers, educating them as to the horrors of street life and the effect that it could have on their kids. Working closely with the Youth for Christ project for girls in Durban and the social workers that they have supplied to the street team, we have been able to change the pattern of inevitable progression to street life for many of these girls. Some of the girls have become members of the YFC shelter while maintaining very strong links with their mothers. These girls range between the ages of four and thirteen.

Specific relationship-building activities have given a strong and solid grounding for the in-depth work to begin. Christmas 1998 was a key time for these activities and, with the help of financial backing from some St Saviour's, Guildford church members, we were able to set up a great programme. The team and I were able to give the street kids Christmas parties, barbecues, beach trips, Christmas meals, soccer championships against the projects and a number of other special treats. These events were instrumental in introducing the children on the streets to the new street team. Many of the events took place at the shelters which gave the kids a brilliant introduction to life away from the streets and the fun that can be had at the shelters.

As well as building relationships with the kids, we used the Christmas activities as a way of interviewing all of the street kids and opening up files on each child to enable us to monitor them on the streets. This documentation is an important part of the street team's work as it really helps the projects that take in the children to understand a bit of the history of the child. Alongside the documentation of the children themselves, we are documenting all abuses that come to our attention on the streets and we are trying to follow up on each one. This may make the security guard, the shopkeeper or the police officer think twice before beating up a child, and might cause the sex abuser to flee in fear of exposure.

During Greenbelt 98, while talking with some of the representatives of Casa Alianza, I heard of how Bruce Harris and Casa Alianza had set up legal advice offices in various different cities in Guatamala and Honduras, specifically to deal with abuse against street children. This is a superb way of fighting powerfully against abuse and an example to the rest of the world. Bruce's experience with street children is second to none, and when organisations are clearly further down the road in their work we do well to take their advice. Although finances are the main obstacle, to open a legal advice centre specifically for the street children would certainly make an issue of the abuses, raise public awareness and perhaps help to initiate some form of justice. Casa Alianza actually documents every single instance of abuse or crime against street children and follows each one up. This does not always get results from the judicial system but at least nothing goes unnoticed and it is a positive step in the identifying of human rights abuses against children.

A street team could also advise compassionate members of the public on how to get involved in supporting the various street children projects and could facilitate local volunteers. A team of this nature may help a city or a town to put street children slightly higher on the welfare priority list. As our street team continues to monitor the streets we hope to be able to break down the lure of street life and eventually to get all of the children off the streets. We hope to be a practical watchdog on the streets and a recognised force of support for children at risk. We can become a visible, practical force on the streets that starts tackling the problem as soon as the children arrive.

There are many advantages to a team such as this and probably the most important is that it can identify children at risk as soon as they arrive on the streets, thus lowering the risk factors of street life and their effect on the future of the children. When small children arrive on the streets they often do not know what they are coming to, they are simply escaping their environment. If there is a better alternative on arrival it will save them becoming street children and it will also improve the chances of them being placed back with their parents if this is an option.

The faster we get children off the streets the lower the risk of them becoming infected with HIV, the less chance of them being emotionally and psychologically destroyed through abuse, the less chance of them being murdered or beaten on the streets, the less chance of them turning to a life of crime or prostitution, the less chance of them becoming physically and mentally destroyed through glue. All that the streets do is to reinforce and create more of the baggage that they arrived on the streets with.

Another obvious effect of a street team is to provide a voice for the children while they are on the streets. It is important to remember that a child does not necessarily make the move to a project overnight. However, they still need a voice and they still have rights while living in the streets. At the moment the streets are like an abyss of lawlessness with street children being the most vulnerable and they need protection while at this stage. Another positive aspect is that the street team will develop an understanding of street life which at the moment is quite literally a whole string of rumours, news articles and horror stories without real recognition of the fundamental components.

The public really doesn't know what happens on the streets. You hear people say, 'They sniff glue, don't they?' or 'They all break into cars', or 'I bet they get abused on the streets', or 'Do you think that they are suffering from AIDS?', or 'Surely they are too young to be involved in prostitution?' The street team can clearly define to the public what the nitty-gritty issues are of living as a street child, while backing it up with real statistics and records of street incidents.

Our street team in Durban is made up of Christians and non-Christians; it is inclusive. This structure is not necessarily bound to be run by Christians, which is why I have so far left out references to spiritual development. However, it is my thinking that what has been described – if carried out

in the right way – would be a very spiritual experience
indeed and would rely heavily on the Holy Spirit for his
power, vitality, energy, charisma, protection, compassion
and servant's heart. It could be a way to develop a Christ-
like approach to the street children in any given city, where
ministry becomes incarnate. Working with the children, the
street-workers can look very closely at how to find a unique
spirituality in street life, particularly as this will not be the
same as that experienced in more stable environments.

If we look at spirituality in what I would term 'the
minimalist way' – as Christians so often do, confining
the Holy Spirit to church services, certain denominations,
Christian jargon and accepted visual results – I feel that we
miss out on the 'God with us' aspect of the faith. If we look
at Christ at work, it was in those everyday experiences,
chance (or not so chance) meetings as well as at organised
gatherings that the miracles and teaching took place. Jesus
developed relationships with those that society considered
the lowest of the low without condemning them. Street
children are often considered the lowest of the low. Perhaps
a team like this can try and use Jesus's approach of
unconditional love.

The team could also involve specific Christian activities
such as starting prayer groups on the streets. I've never seen
this before. Wouldn't it be great? This, of course, would
have to be continued at the projects as well with their
permission, and if done in a non-dominant, non-aggressive
and humble way should not pose a problem. The possibilities are endless for the street team. Imagine having the local
churches involved, with the team providing facilities for fun
activities, spiritual development programmes, Sunday
school and other resources. They could encourage the
children by inviting them to services, welcoming them with
open arms. Imagine having church-backed, interdenomina-
tional fund-raising awareness days for the greater street
children structures; in other words, the projects. Imagine

making street children one of the top priorities for the Christians in a certain area – this could be dynamic. It could change the whole town's thinking towards street children. It could trigger an awakening.

I pray that the street team of Durban may continue to be an agent of unification and an encouragement to the projects and organisations concerned with street children in that city, as it continues on its journey attempting to provide the missing link.

13   Reflections

My favourite haunt in Durban is a little coffee shop run by
surfers on the beach, where I can sit in the front yard under
the palm trees watching my favourite surfing spot: 'New
Pier'. Durban is a wonderful city – the beaches are superb,
the weather is warm and the sea is like a bath. It is truly a
beautiful place with wonderful sunrises over the sea and
sunsets over the city.

My life of working with the street children has become
intertwined with my surfing. Obviously, surfing takes a
back seat but I've been very fortunate to have been able
to surf some of the best waves in the world. I have spent
time at the world-renowned surfing venue, Jeffries Bay
(J-Bay) famed for its classic, hollow, ongoing waves called
'super tubes'. I have also surfed extensively around the
Natal and Eastern Cape Coast. I surf every day, not
competitively, just for fun. I have really enjoyed the beauty
of the South African coastline and the quality of surf.
There's nothing better than a six- to eight-foot swell
with a light offshore wind, especially when the 'tubes' are
plentiful!

I have recently started surfing netted beaches but only
after the recent rise in shark attacks. I have seen sharks and
I do not fancy becoming lunch, I still have work to do.
Fortunately Durban's beaches have shark nets so I don't
have to worry too much about this now. Recently I broke
my foot landing a surfing manoeuvre and had to sit out for
six weeks, which was more painful than the break itself!
I thank God for the gift of a hobby like surfing and also
thank him for putting it in perspective for me. Surfing is my

hobby, my way of relaxing, but not my life. It is a great way of enjoying God's creation.

Durban is changing and there is a new up-and-coming crew of black surfers emerging. They are starting to get sponsors and encouragement from the local surfing industry and are proving to be very talented. I am sure the number of black surfers on Durban city beaches will increase over the next five years and this will be great. It is exciting to see the changing environment touching sports like surfing which have, up until now, been almost exclusively white in South Africa.

As I paddle out into the sea on my surfboard at five o'clock in the morning, the sun is rising and I'm overcome with the beauty of God's creation. I take off on a good size wave, bottom turn and push back up to lip. I can't help but feel that I'm not the only one playing in the waves; I know that God is enjoying himself too as I enjoy his creation. It is at times like this that I am able to see God's wonder and taste his splendour a little. At times like this I know that he is in total control over my life; I feel rejuvenated. Often I pray in the surf and it seems a far cry from the hustle and bustle of city life just one block away.

I thank God at these times for looking after me during the last six years and for the joy of working with street children. As I walk across the beach back to my flat with the morning sun warm on my back I often think of all the children that I've known over the years. I often ponder over what the last six and a half years have done to my life. I remember the children now living with new hope and those who still wait. Sometimes I feel tired, older than my years. I've seen things that have impacted me deeply and have broken my heart, then rebuilt it to be twice as strong. I've wept and cried out to God; I've wrestled with the way of Christ.

One girl that I am working with at the time of writing has just turned fifteen although she looks about twelve or thirteen. This girl has AIDS. She has suffered the abuse of the streets since the age of eleven being used in prostitution. She is such a lovely child yet she will die within the next year or so. She never stood a chance. As we try and give her quality of life in her final days the horror of the situation stares us in the eyes. However, she does matter; her life does mean something and God is with her.

I've cried with the kids and laughed with them, reprimanded them and fought for them. I've been in scary situations. I have looked down the barrel of a gun twice while sticking up for the kids and had a knife up against my throat. I have seen violence. I watched someone being shot in the head from point-blank range while I was standing six feet away. I have watched a number of street shoot-outs and seen countless stabbings. I've come into contact with more rape victims than I can possibly remember and have watched children die in the streets. I have lost loved ones to the streets and have watched friends live and die with AIDS. I've become a target for personal persecution constantly from certain peoples for speaking up and have suffered defamation of character as well as being beaten up.

Sometimes I wonder what I am supposed to do with these experiences. How are they supposed to shape my life? I know that God's protection has been with me over the years; this much is obvious. I have seen God at work in the lives of hundreds of children constantly through this period and although I have seen so many negatives, God's power outweighs them massively. I come away from all this knowing that God is in control. However, it has made me reconsider interpretations of Christ and what it is to be a Christian.

I am really grateful for my many experiences in South Africa. I have been fortunate enough to watch history in the making as the new South Africa unfolds. It has been wonderful to be with the street children through such a historic time. The children have brought me much joy over the years. There have been many precious moments.

I have watched the children proudly from the audience as they perform in school plays. I remember one girl called Zanyiwe who was in a local school production and had a walk-on part with one line. From the moment she walked on the stage to the moment she walked off she stared directly into my eyes, making sure I was watching the whole time. It was as if I was the only person in the audience and she was proudly performing for me.

Small things have been wonderful, like the time that I returned from a brief trip to England to find the hall at Isaiah 58 decorated with the words, 'Welcome home, Tom, we love you.' It has been fantastic to watch the children overcome their situation, identifying their strengths and utilising them. One boy at Daily Bread called Lindile has a proven talent for acting and has excelled in local productions. He is an actor of quality and is learning to master his gift. Seeing the children's many talents coming out at Daily Bread has left me with many cherished memories. The 'gum boot dancers', six boys with the most unbelievable talent and co-ordination who have mastered the traditional South African mineworkers' dance is one of my favourites.

Nothing describes the elation when one of the boys passes his driving test after training hard in difficult circumstances. One boy at Daily Bread called Stanley passed his driving test after a couple of attempts and this opened up many job opportunities for him. It was a great moment when he found out that he had passed and had added such an achievement to his name.

The joy of watching the children acquire new hope is awesome. Most recently, while writing this book, I have seen a boy called Wiseman reunited with his family after three years on the streets. I worked with him for a month to reach this stage and it was wonderful to see him overcome his situation. He is like a new child now.

Another boy whose nickname was 'Msotho' because he had come from the Orange Free State where the language is

'SeSotho' had run away from the little town of Bethlehem – not the famous one where Jesus was born, though! He came from Bethlehem in the Orange Free State, and had run away to Durban. He had become so addicted to glue that he could no longer walk any more and was desperate to return home to get away from street life. However, he had no means now. I took him back to his home where his mother promptly broke down in tears, saying that she had been looking for him for so long. She had the means to support him but could not find him. He now lives at home where he is away from the glue and his legs will slowly recover. He started school again in January 1999.

I'm twenty-seven now. My first twenty years were spent submerged in Western culture with a deep interest in other cultures around the world. My time in South Africa has predominantly been spent in a completely different culture. What this means is that out of my adult years from the age of eighteen I have spent two years in my original culture and almost seven out of it. It has been a very interesting spiritual journey for me and I feel particularly challenged at the moment as to what I believe. I have found myself asking new questions, especially concerning our Western interpretation of biblical events.

It has caused me to start yearning to read the Bible again, contextualising it, researching the culture of the time and then looking at how it would be applicable in different cultures today. I am no expert on this but I think that this may give me new insight into the way of Christ and how it can be applicable to my journey. If you use a computer you will know that 'text only' is the basic original document in a particular format. Once you put this document into word-processing software like Microsoft Word it remains the same work but takes on the character of the software. In other words, it is alive within the programme. Different cultures, I believe, are like these programmes with God's truth, 'the text', being applicable to all. However, the truth will always look a little different on the outside in different cultures but the core will always be the same.

I'm completely at ease with who I am, my colour and roots, and I thank God for this as I recognise that all colours and peoples are made in his image. I am quite happy to play my part in the rainbow but I also thank God for the opportunity to diversify, grow and continue shaping my identify as I go through life.

I now speak Xhosa and feel that I understand more and love the people. The Xhosas have taught me much and I love some of their value systems and traditions. They have been extremely welcoming to me and I remain indebted to them for their hospitality, love and vibrancy. Living among Xhosas has challenged many of my Western values. For one thing, I've become kind of used to people greeting each other! In all my time of working on the streets I've never experienced racism against me, and local people have come and encouraged me in my work on the streets. Many of them never knew how they have fuelled my fire.

'The young people are the future' is a clichéd expression often used to sell a way of thinking to the youth or to market a product, but in essence it is true. What I would like to see most is a mobilised, radical youth movement seeking social justice, full of budding activists. If the older generation is not interested in standing with us then we are strong enough to fight ourselves. We have the power, but not always the wisdom that comes with time and experience. Young people must be ready to stand up. In the struggle in South Africa, the youth played a major part: the ANC youth league, the PAC youth league, schoolchildren and the youth in general brought the struggle forward and sometimes died for it. Whereas our struggles may not be as horrific as the apartheid struggle we need to take a stand and be ready and committed as youth and young people.

We need to be political and vocal, and if we feel that we personally have no struggle then we need to help someone else fight their struggle. Campaign against Third World debt, against inner-city racism, support the Palestinians and the Israeli peacemakers, fight sexism, encourage prison inmates, fight child abuse, help fight AIDS and care for those living with the disease, raise support for street child projects, campaign against child labour, encourage victims of divorce, feed the homeless, talk to the homeless, *do* something! There is a world of sorrow out there and you have a chance, whoever you are, wherever you are, to be an activist and to be a shining beacon of encouragement. You too will need encouragers in your low moments.

Giving to charities is often something we young people leave to the oldies – forget that. No matter how little money we earn or how much (!) we have a responsibility to our brothers and sisters in the global community. Dig deep, free yourself from the shackles of social inactivity (or too much social activity, depending on the context!).

I am happy to hold on to the 'text' and enjoy the spiritual exploration. I cannot fully describe the joy in finding new evidence of God's character, artistry, love and compassion, whether it be in meeting new people, appreciating his creation or contemplating his word. On finding new evidence or another piece to the puzzle one often wants to pause for a moment, revel in it, flirt with it, taste it and soak in it.

In surf language it is like discovering a new surf spot, and wanting to enjoy the perfect waves. These waves are so beautiful, so round and so new; the surfer just wants to stay in the water and bask in the glory. When the surfer finally gets out of the water the memory of the event is lodged deep in his mind and the experience helps shape his future surfing.

I am fascinated by Jesus because every person that has impressed me with their life has had Christ-like qualities. To me Jesus is radical, on the edge, going against the flow, not afraid to stand up, even to be killed. Jesus was not just this, otherwise he may as well have been just a soldier. He was love personified, a champion of peace, a saviour for the oppressed, the poor and the fallen.

If all Christians tried to emulate the real Jesus this world would be a different place. Christianity has no boundaries. Christians need to be political, ethical, radical and determined to make real progress along the road. Confining Christianity to certain safe areas is marginalising Christ. It was Desmond Tutu who said, 'I am puzzled about which Bible people are reading when they suggest religion and politics don't mix.' I believe that this is a profound statement.

Not everybody needs to get up and go halfway around the world, as there are plenty of needs in every area. We need to mobilise youth in our home areas as well and encourage each other in our individual callings to be part of the community. I encourage much prayer and asking for wisdom as you explore the area of social justice.

If you're one of the growing number of young people ready to give a 'year of your life' and really want to visit, learn from, serve and encourage other communities, please remember the golden rule. Find a good organisation in keeping with your radical thinking that will point you in the right direction. Never just get up and go because it is a dangerous world with much to be done and time-wasting is not needed. Do not put yourself in harm's way, you are too valuable.

There are brilliant organisations in the UK and the rest of the world where you will be trained, fine-tuned and guided as you embark on making a difference. You need to be equipped to make a difference. There are plenty of people in the West Bank and Gaza Strip, plenty in Soweto, plenty in Rio de Janeiro, Manila and Kampala. Make sure that you're not just going out to these places presuming that your Western presence will somehow make a difference. Be trained to serve.

It is fine to go on holiday to South Africa, now sanctions are over. I encourage you if you are able – I say 'able' because it costs an arm and a leg – then go, the South African economy needs your money. But please contact an organisation which can help you to get the whole picture when out there. It is not all about security fences, beaches, swimming pools, Mercedes, rock and roll, barbecues, cricket and rugby. It is really about vibrant community life, poverty, joy in hardship, *kwaito* (local) music, gospel music, taxis, dusty townships, hospitality, soccer, boxing, shebeens (usually unlicensed township bars) and *mqombothi* (African beer).

In 1990 I remember being part of my first Amos Trust trip in South Africa. I remember meeting people who were committed to making a difference. I also remember the night when I saw street children for the first time with the bishop and my father in Mozambique. That trip changed my life.

During my time at the Amos Trust I have come to see the trust as a big global family comprising the partners, supporters, fieldworkers, trustees and staff. It is a family committed to social justice. I have become very aware of the important role that the supporters play in the work that I do – it is a partnership. I have been very fortunate to have a wonderful support base in the UK comprising individuals, churches, home groups and schools. Without these people I would certainly not have been able to complete the last six years' work. I am indebted to and eternally grateful for all those that have prayed for me, all those who have supported the work financially and all those who have encouraged me along the way. I have two grandmothers who pray for me daily; for my safety, my work and of course for the kids. To them I am really thankful.

The Amos Trust started as an organisation that supported my father on his travels to forgotten communities around the world to bring a message of reconciliation and hope. My father is still director of Amos Trust and is Guild vicar of All Hallows on the Wall in London Wall Road where the Amos offices are situated. He also leads Christian Aid's London and South East team from offices on the other side of the church! The church has indeed become a centre for issues of social justice.

The Amos Trust continues to grow as a voice for the voiceless and I continue to work on the streets with the street children of South Africa. As long as there are still Mduduzas, Siphokazis and Sisekos we as a global community still have a huge responsibility, and I will continue to fight for the rights of street children and to tell their stories.

My prayer for South Africa and indeed for the street children of that country is linked in with the Amos Trust vision and appears in the Bible in Amos 5: 24: 'But let justice roll on like a river, righteousness like a never-failing stream!'

A few days after the 1994 general election, when the results came out, there was a party atmosphere with cars hooting, singing and general elation. It was great, the townships were alive. Later that day I went for a surf on the main East London beach where I sat and contemplated the beauty of the event. As I watched from the sea, I saw a crowded beachfront and listened to endless singing and horns blaring. As I sat on my surfboard, soaking in the atmosphere, I noticed another white surfer put his hands to his mouth and shout towards the beach 'f***ing kaffirs'. His words were drowned out by the roar of the waves.

I looked at him, then looked at the beach and thought to myself, 'You've had your day. Your loud voice has been taken away. Nobody will hear your cry.' I then smiled to myself, and paddled off to catch a wave. The new South Africa had been born.

To support Tom's work on the streets of Durban
and to receive our regular news letter,
please contact the Amos Trust at the address below.

Amos supports Tom's work by looking after his expenses
and by giving directly to the work with the children. If you
would like to be part of this, then please contact Beki at the
Amos office.

Amos Trust
All Hallows on the Wall
83 London Wall
London
EC2M 5ND
Tel: 0171 588 2661/2638
Fax: 0171 588 2663
Email: amos_trust@compuserve.com
Website: http://www.onthewall.org

About the Amos Trust

Amos Trust was originally set up to support Tom's father,
singer Garth Hewitt's, trips to Third World countries. It has
now developed into a small agency, supporting work in five
areas of the world, with a commitment to raising an
awareness of justice issues among people in the UK.

South Africa
Amos on the Streets
supports Tom Hewitt in his work with street children in
Durban.

Uganda
Taata Project
works closely with those suffering from HIV/AIDS and the
many children who are orphaned as a result. As well as
pastoral care and health promotion, Taata funds the education and welfare of more than 150 children.

Palestine-Israel
a) *Al Alhi Arab Hospital*
situated in Gaza, is the only privately run public hospital in
the area, providing vital health care services.

b) *Open House*
a reconciliation initiative in Ramle, provides nursery facilities for Palestinian children. It also runs summer camps for
Jewish and Palestinian teenagers and works with adults
towards better cultural understanding.

Nicaragua
a) *Avocado Tree School*
is situated in La Concepcion, a very poor town in the heart
of the Nicaraguan countryside. At Avocado our support
helps to pay the salaries of teachers, as well as providing
support for those children whose families cannot afford to
pay tuition fees of £1.60 per month.

b) *Honduras and Nicaragua*
Since the devastation in Central America caused by Hurri-
cane Mitch in November '98, we continue to send funds to
our partners in Honduras and Nicaragua to help in the
rebuilding of their communities.

Philippines
a) *Mango Tree House*
in Manila, is home to thirty-five children with a committed team
who feed, clothe, educate, and genuinely love these former
street kids. Mango also supports thirty-five students outside the
home by providing school fees, uniforms and books.

b) *Cashew Tree House*
operates as a pre-school for forty-five young children from the
Payatas rubbish dump in Manila and the surrounding streets.
It also offers community services for families from the area.

Amos also places an emphasis on Human Rights and continues to organise Garth Hewitt's trips and concerts (those not directly related to Christian Aid)

Human Rights
At present we are highlighting the cases of Irene Fernandez in Malaysia and Modechi Vananu in Israel which we will continue to pursue until they are resolved.

The Collective
is a vibrant network for those in their twenties and thirties who are interested in making the hopeful nature of the gospel a reality. Every three months we meet to hear various speakers, obtain detailed updates on the projects, learn from our partners, and to pray. If you would like to be part of a radical and mobilised group of young adults then *The Collective* is for you.

If you would like to be kept informed about the ongoing work of Amos, or would like information about regular giving, please contact the Amos Trust at the address on the previous page.

☉⊕☉ amos trust

justice and hope for the forgotten

Registered charity 292592